AH-64 APACHE

in action

By Al Adcock

Color by Don Greer
Illustrated by Perry Manley

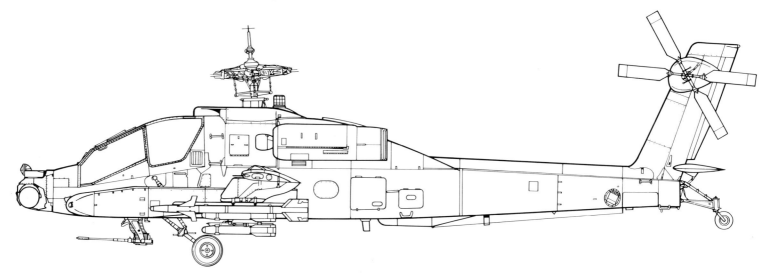

Aircraft Number 95
squadron/signal publications

An AH-64A Apache of the 2nd Squadron, 6th Air Cavalry, VII Corps Aviation Brigade flies a patrol near its home base of Isselheim, West Germany. Apaches form an important part of NATO anti-armor forces in Germany.

ISBN 0-89747-223-3

If you have any photographs of the aircraft, armor, soldiers or ships of any nation, particularly wartime snapshots, why not share them with us and help make Squadron/Signal's books all the more interesting and complete in the future. Any photograph sent to us will be copied and the original returned. The donor will be fully credited for any photos used. Please send them to:

Squadron/Signal Publications, Inc.
1115 Crowley Drive.
Carrollton, TX 75011-5010.

Acknowledgements

I would like to thank the following people at Fort Rucker, Alabama for their help: LTCOL Steve Rausch (Commanding Officer 1st Battalion, 212th Aviation Regiment), LTCOL Daniel J. Boccolucci (Commanding Officer 1st Battalion 14th Aviation Regiment), Bill Hayes, CAPT Steve Huyett, SP4 Frank Sullivan, and Betty Goodson of the Army Public Affairs Office; Tim Edwards and Jim Craig at the U.S. Army Aviation Museum; Merle Clapsaddle of the Army Aviation Test Activity, CW4 Joe Decurtis and George Fabian at the Army Aviation Learning Center; S/SGT Ben Goneberg and Bill Kyser at the AH-64 Combat Mission Simulator, and John Daves at the Photo Lab. A very special thanks to Jim Ramsey and Bill Crouch of McDonnell Douglas Helicopter. I promise not to bother them again until I write about another MDHC product.

Photo Credits

Garth Adcock
Lockheed
Harry Baldwin
Grumman
Singer-Link
Teledyne-Ryan
U.S. Navy
U.S. Army
U.S. Air Force
China Clipper Photography

Apache Magazine
Western Design
Martin Marietta
General Dynamics
GM-Hughes Aircraft
Bell Helicopter
Rockwell International
Ford Aerospace
McDonnell Douglas Helicopter
Peter Harlem

An AH-64A Apache of the 6th Cavalry Brigade flies over one of the Fort Hood, Texas, practice ranges. The Apache is the Army's first line anti-armor attack helicopter and is the best anti-armor attack helicopter in the World today. (U.S. Army)

Introduction

The AH-64 Apache is the latest in a long line of armed rotary wing aircraft that dates back to the Second World War when the Focke-Achgelis Fa 223 was armed with a 7.7MM MG 15 machine gun. Early helicopters were envisioned for use in the search and rescue role where they were likely to encounter the enemy and armament was included for self defense. It wasn't until the Korean War (1950-1953) that serious consideration was given to using the helicopter as an offensive platform armed with guns and rockets.

The Bell H-13 was the first American helicopter to be armed with machine guns for self defense. Later, Sikorsky H-34s and Piasecki H-21s were armed with rockets as well as guns and this practice led to the beginnings of the true armed attack helicopter. During 1954, the U.S. Army, based on its experience in the Korean War, saw the need for a dedicated armed helicopter that could escort troop-carrying helicopters and could suppress enemy ground fire. The armed helicopter would also have the capability to go deep into enemy territory, perform its rescue mission and return. With these missions in mind the Army developed several armed helicopters including the UH-1 Huey gunship and AH-1 Huey Cobra.

The armed attack helicopter concept came into its own and grew during the Vietnam War (1961-1972). The primary armed helicopter early in the war was the Bell UH-1 Huey. Originally, armed versions of the Huey carried four M60 machine guns and rockets. Army use of these helicopters drew heavy criticism from the U.S. Air Force which viewed the armed helicopter as an encroachment into their territory of air support for ground forces. The debate between the Army and Air Force had started during the Korean War and became heated during Vietnam.

Pressures from the war forced a compromise between the Air Force and Army, resulting in the Key West Agreements of 1966. The Army gave the Air Force their CV-2 Caribou transports and in return the Army was allowed to pursue development of the helicopter gunship to support ground troops in the air mobile role. By the end of the Vietnam War, various Huey variants had been armed with 7.62MM six barrel mini-guns, 2.75 inch rockets, TOW anti-tank missiles, .50 caliber machine guns, 40MM grenade launchers, and 20MM cannons.

The first dedicated armed attack helicopter to enter Army service was the Bell AH-1 Huey Cobra. The Cobra utilized the engine, rotor system and drive system of the Huey, and mating it to an all new fuselage that featured tandem seating, and stub wings. The Cobra was armed with 2.75 inch rockets, a 40MM grenade launcher, and M60 machine guns. With its slim fuselage, the Cobra had far greater speed and maneuverability than the Huey. The tandem cockpit gave the crew, pilot and copilot/gunner, greater visibility for spotting and attacking targets. The Huey Cobra proved to be a huge success since it carried enough armament to be an effective ground support aircraft and it freed up the Huey fleet for their intended role of troop carrier. The Cobra, however, had a number of limitations. The Cobra's single Lycoming T-53 engine did not produce enough power to be able to handle the hot weather conditions in Vietnam and a full armament load at the same time. While good, the Cobra was not the aircraft the Army needed for its future wars.

During June of 1963, the Army began a program, known as the Fire Support Aerial System, to identify the operational requirements of its next generation of attack helicopter. During 1964, the program was redesignated the Advanced Aerial Fire Support System (AAFSS) and a Request for Proposals (RFP) was issued to interested companies for an advanced armed attack helicopter. After evaluating proposals from both Lockheed and Sikorsky, the Army announced that Lockheed had won with its technologically advanced Lockheed AH-56 Cheyenne.

The AH-56 was powered by a 3,435 shp General Electric turboshaft engine and had a projected top speed of 250 mph. Highly advanced, the Cheyenne utilized a rigid rotor system and a pusher propeller for increased forward thrust. During 1969 after the Army had procured and tested ten Cheyenne prototypes, a decision was made to cancel the entire project. Tests had revealed that the Cheyenne was too complicated to maintain in the field and it had become far too costly to build. The original projected per unit cost was to have been 1.2 million dollars; however, project cost overruns had driven the per unit cost to over 2 million dollars each by the time the project was finally cancelled.

Experience in Vietnam with the Huey Cobra, along with Air Force pressure, forced a change in Army thinking about the role of the armed helicopter in future combat. This change in policy brought about the advanced attack helicopter (AAH) program during 1972. There were two basic requirements specified in the Request For Proposals issued by the Army for the AAH. One requirement covered the aircraft's mission capabilities and the other identified specific equipment that was to be used in the aircraft's design. The mission statement specified that the new attack helicopter was to be an integrated weapons system with a primary role of anti-armor attack. The aircraft was to be capable of operations during all types of weather, day and night, over all types of terrain. The second part of the Army requirement stated that the new aircraft was to be powered by two 1,536 shp General Electric T-700 turboshaft engines and be armed with a 30MM cannon for both anti-armor and suppressive fire.

The Lockheed YAH-56 Cheyenne was built to replace the AH-1 Cobra; however, development problems and severe cost overruns led to the project being cancelled during 1972. Fast and heavily armed, the Cheyenne had a performance close to that of a fighter aircraft. (Lockheed)

A total of five companies responded to the RFP; Bell, Boeing Vertol, Lockheed, Hughes, and Sikorsky. On 22 June 1972, two companies, Hughes Helicopter (Model 77) and Bell Helicopter (Model 409), were awarded contracts to build a static test airframe and two flying prototypes. The Bell Model 409 received the designation YAH-63 and the Hughes Model 77 was designated the YAH-64.

Bell's YAH-63 prototype flew on 1 October 1975; however, it crashed on 4 June 1976 just before it was to be turned over to the Army for evaluation. Rebuilt and delivered to the Army, it was evaluated for four months during 1976. At the end of the evaluation the Army stated that the aircraft was of little or no improvement over the AH-1 Cobra. The YAH-63 had used an airframe and rotor system based largely on the Model 309 King Cobra (an updated Huey Cobra). Bell's decision to use a two bladed main and tail rotor, plus reversing the seating arrangement for the crew, putting the pilot up front and the copilot/gunner in the rear, effectively eliminated the Bell entry from contention.

First flown on 30 September 1975, the Hughes YAH-64 (Hughes company designation AV-02; (AV-01 was the ground test vehicle entry in the AAH program took an entirely different approach. The YAH-64 prototypes (AV-02 and AV-03) emerged as twin engined, four bladed main rotor, four bladed tail rotor, two place helicopters, with the engines mounted in pods alongside the fuselage above the two stub wings. The prototype featured sharply swept back main landing gear legs and a free-swiveling, lockable tail wheel. The crew was housed in a tandem cockpit with conventional co-pilot/gunner and pilot seating (i.e. gunner in front, pilot in back). Access to the cockpit was made through opening canopy panels on the starboard side of the aircraft. Above the tail rotor was installed a T style horizontal stabilizer. The stub wings were configured with four weapons pylons and the secondary gun armament was installed under the forward fuselage in an unfaired turret. The weapons sighting system (either a Northrop or Martin Marietta system) was to be installed at the extreme nose once final selection on which system would be used was made.

Hughes also designed the prototype to feature a number of design innovations in the areas of servicability and maintainability. The main landing gear was designed to be capable of being lowered, making maintenance easier. Engine access panels were stressed to also serve as work platforms for maintenance crews. The forty-eight foot fully articulated four blade main rotor and eight foot, four inch scissors type four blade tail rotor were designed to be capable of withstanding anti-aircraft hits of up to 23MM and still function.

The YAH-64 was selected by the Army as the winner after the Phase I flyoff between it and the Bell YAH-63. The formal announcement was made by the Secretary of the Army on 10 December 1976. Phase II of the contract required the manufacture of three additional prototypes for avionics and weapons testing.

The Bell YAH-63 was one of the entries in the Army's AAH (Advanced Attack Helicopter) competition. The Bell Model 409 reversed the standard placement of pilot and gunner by having the gunner occupy the rear cockpit. In the event, the Bell entry lost the contract to the Hughes YAH-64. (Bell Helicopter)

The Hughes YAH-64 (73-22248) prototype made its first flight on 30 September 1975. The early YAH-64 prototypes featured a high T tail plane, and straight tipped rotor blades. The probe mounted on the port side of the nose was a test air data probe. (McDonnell-Douglas)

Development

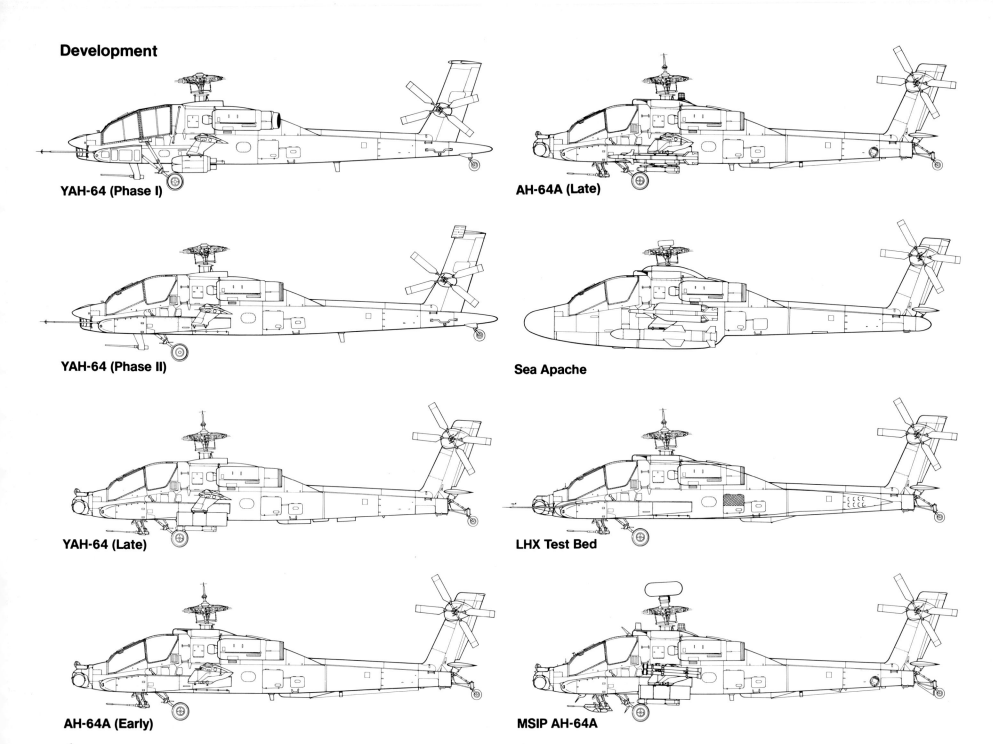

YAH-64 (Phase I)

AH-64A (Late)

YAH-64 (Phase II)

Sea Apache

YAH-64 (Late)

LHX Test Bed

AH-64A (Early)

MSIP AH-64A

Phase II YAH-64

The fifty-six month Phase II portion of the AAH program began during January of 1977 and called for the construction of three additional full scale development prototypes. These three (AV-04, AV-05, AV-06), like the first prototypes, were built at the Hughes facility at Culver City, California. Prior to beginning the Phase II tests a number of modifications were made to the first three prototypes.

The main rotor blades received swept tips replacing the original squared-off tips, the rotor mast height was increased by six inches, and the tail rotor diameter was increased by three inches. In an attempt to cure dynamic load problems that had been encountered during Phase I tests, the tail plane of prototype AV-02 was altered with a reverse taper and end plates being fitted to the stabilizer tips. Prototype AV-03 was also modified with entended fuselage cheek fairings to cover the enlarged avionics bays and the canopy was altered with the flat glass side panels being replaced by bulged panels.

Originally, the Army had planned to arm the YAH-64 with the TOW anti-tank missile system. In the event, the Rockwell Hellfire anti-armor missile development had proceeded far faster than anticipated and it became the weapon of choice. On 18 March 1979, YAH-64 AV-02 successfully fired the Hellfire missile for the first time at Camp Pendleton, California.

During Phase II testing, the prototypes were required to demonstrate their ability to perform the aircraft's primary mission for the U.S. Army. One of the requirements was that the AH-64, armed with eight Hellfire missiles, 320 rounds of 30MM ammunition and with enough fuel for 1.83 hours flight time demonstrate a minimum 450 feet per minute vertical rate of climb at 95 percent engine power under hot and high conditions (based on a standard Army hot day of 95° Fahrenheit at 4,000 feet). Not only did the YAH-64 meet the minimum requirements, it exceeded them by a factor of three. The rate of climb, based on actual flight test data, was 1,450 feet per minute.

To be effective on the battle field, a weapon system such as the Apache must be able to survive battle damage. To meet Army survivability requirements, the airframe, engines, transmission and rotor blades were constructed to withstand hits of 12.7MM and survive hits up to 23MM and still function. The crew and cockpit area was given special consideration with light weight Kevlar armor being placed in strategic locations. To further enhance crew survivability a transparent blast shield was placed between the pilot and copilot/gunner.

On 31 October 1979, prototype AV-04 was completed. This aircraft incorporated a number of modifications to the tail section that had been dictated by problems encountered with the first three prototypes. The original T tail was replaced by a low mounted one piece horizontal stabilator. This stabilator cut down on dynamic vibrations and gave the YAH-64 much better low speed control. Besides relocating the stabilator, Hughes also raised the height of the vertical fin slightly and repositioned the tail rotor and gear box assembly to a position two and a half feet higher on the vertical fin and slightly forward. The diameter of the tail rotor was also increased. The two remaining prototypes were also built with this new tail configuration and the earlier prototypes were modified to this standard during overhauls.

Between the years 1979 and 1983, the Apache logged over 4,000 hours of flight testing and gave numerous flight demonstrations. During 1981 the Army, in keeping with its policy to name its helicopters after North American Indian tribes, bestowed the name Apache on the YAH-64. During this period the Apache was evaluated by the U.S. Marine Corps as a possible successor to the AH-IT Sea Cobra. During 1982, one of the Apache prototypes conducted a tour of NATO countries in an attempt to sell the AH-64 to allied air forces. The test program suffered one setback when prototype AV-04 was destroyed in a mid-air collision with a T-28 chase plane.

When Hughes had received the contract to build the YAH-64 prototypes, they realized that their facilities at Culver City would be inadequate to handle full scale production. A decision was made to construct a new manufacturing facility for the helicopter in an area free from the congested traffic of Los Angeles.

The new Hughes facility was built at Mesa, Arizona with construction beginning on 5 March 1982. When completed, the new facility was the most modern helicopter production complex ever built, containing some 550,000 square feet of work area. The first Hughes employees moved into the new facility during February of 1983, ready to begin production of the Apache.

In March of 1983, after some ten years of design and testing, the Defense Systems Acquisitions Review Council gave its final approval to the Apache and ordered the aircraft into production under the designation AH-64A.

YAH-64 prototypes, AV-01 and AV-02 (73-22248 and 73-22249), were initially equipped with TOW anti-tank missile launchers. Originally, the Army specified that the TOW was to be the anti-armor missile carried by the Apache; however, the TOW was later superseded by the superior Hellfire missile. (U.S. Army)

The third YAH-64 prototype, AV-03 (Air Vehicle 03, 77-23256) was configured with Hellfire anti-tank missiles on modular launchers. The early prototypes featured a T-tail horizontal stabilizer configuration and flat sided canopies. (U.S. Army)

The second YAH-64 prototype (AV-02 73-22249) was the first to actually fire a Hellfire missile. The first launch took place during missile firing trials held at Camp Pendleton, California. The 30mm cannon under the fuselage was a dummy installation. (McDonnell Douglas)

The Army took the second YAH-64 prototype (77-23259) on a tour of U.S. Armed Forces bases during 1982. At this time the prototype was equipped with early style weapon pylons; however, it had been modified with a number of production features such as a TADS/PNVS turret and ADS sensor on the rotor mast. (U.S. Navy)

Main Rotor Blade Development

**YAH-64
(Early)**

**YAH-64
(Phase II)**

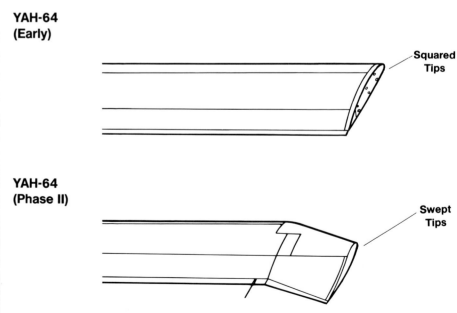

The sixth YAH-64 prototype (AV-06 77-23259) was the first to be fitted with the low mounted stabilator. AV-06 was also fitted with a production TADS/PNVS nose turret, an Air Data Sensor (ADS) probe on the rotor mast above the blades, and extended side sponsons. (Rockwell)

In an attempt to reduce dynamic vibrations in the tail area, the horizontal stabilizer was given a reverse taper and fitted with end plates. This modification did not produce the desired improvement and the tail was later completely redesigned. (U.S. Army)

Prototype YAH-64s not only visited Army installations, but Navy bases such as Naval Air Station Norfolk, Virginia, during 1984. For the tour the prototype was armed with Hellfire missiles and 2.75 inch rocket launchers. (U.S. Navy)

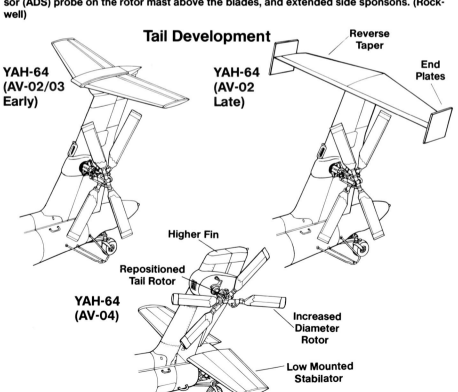

Tail Development

YAH-64
(AV-02/03
Early)

YAH-64
(AV-02
Late)

Reverse Taper

End Plates

Higher Fin

Repositioned Tail Rotor

YAH-64
(AV-04)

Increased Diameter Rotor

Low Mounted Stabilator

AH-64A

During 1982, Hughes received a contract to proceed with production of eleven production aircraft under the designation AH-64A. While final testing was still ongoing, the Army decided to replace the 1,536 shp General Electric T700-GE-700 engine with a more powerful uprated version of the 700 series engine. General Electric had developed this engine for installation in the Sikorsky SH-60 Seahawk for the Navy, and the Army decided to re-engine prototype AV-05 with this powerplant. Tests proved that the new engine was compatible with the Apache airframe and the Army ordered that production Apaches be powered by this 1,723 shp engine under the designation T700-GE-701.

With receipt of the first production contract, Hughes notified Teledyne Ryan in San Diego, California (the sub-contractor responsible for the fuselage, wings, and tail assembly) to proceed with production of the first eleven Apache sub-assemblies. By March of 1983, the first complete fuselage sub-assembly arrived at Mesa and production of the Apache began. The first aircraft (PV-1, i.e. production vehicle number 1) rolled off the Mesa assembly line on 30 September 1983.

Production AH-64As incorporated all the modifications tested on the prototypes. These included the low mounted stabilator, revised canopy, increased diameter tail rotor, taller fin, and enlarged side fuselage avionics bay fairings. Additionally, the nose profile of the production Apache differed considerably from the prototypes due to the installation of a production TADS/PNVS sensor turret. The weapons pylons were also changed with a wider movable pylon replacing the earlier narrow fixed pylons.

The production AH-64A Apache's semi-monocoque fuselage has an overall length of 49 feet 1 inch, a height of 15 feet 3 inches, a width of 9 feet and the wing span of the stub wings is 17 feet 1 inch. The main rotor has a diameter of 48 feet, while the the tail rotor diameter is 9 feet 2 inches. Empty weight is 10,760 pounds while primary mission gross weight is 14,445 pounds and ferry mission (1,000 nautical miles) gross weight is 21,000 pounds, almost double the aircraft's empty weight.

During 1984, Hughes Helicopter was purchased by McDonnell Douglas Aircraft and became McDonnell Douglas Helicopter Company. During that same year, the AH-64A Apache was awarded the National Aeronautics Association 1983 Robert J. Collier Trophy. The Collier Trophy is perhaps the most coveted and prestigious award in aviation for achievements in aeronautics and astronautics.

The Apache was designed from the start to be easily maintained in the field without the aid of separate work stands or ladders. The aircraft is equipped with built-in work platforms, stowable access steps, and easily accessible work areas. One innovation is an on board fault detection/location system that points out on board problems to the ground crews. All of the electric and fluid lines are quick disconnect types which make replacement easy and fast even under field conditions.

The transmission is installed in such a manner that it is removable for quick replacement without having to remove the main rotor mast or main rotor system. The Apache is equipped with an auxiliary power unit (APU) to provide on ground power for all of the extensive electric, hydraulic, and pneumatic systems and acts as a self contained starter unit for the two 1,723 shp T700-GE-701 engines. Maintenance requirements are further reduced by using grease-lubricated (instead of oil) intermediate and tail rotor gear boxes.

The airframe, wings, and engine nacelle assemblies are of semi-monocoque construction and of conventional aircraft grade aluminum for ease of repairs in the field. The fuselage has been designed to survive hits from weapons of 12.7mm up to 23mm, the main types of weapons that are expected to be encountered on the battlefield. The fuselage is also stressed to absorb a vertical impact of forty-two feet per second and still

The first production AH-64A (82-23355) made its first flight on 9 January 1984 with McDonnell Douglas chief experimental pilot Steve Harvey at the controls. Designated the PV-1 (Production Vehicle One) it was the first Apache assembled at the McDonnell Douglas (ex-Hughes) Mesa, Arizona, facility. (McDonnell Douglas)

Nose Development

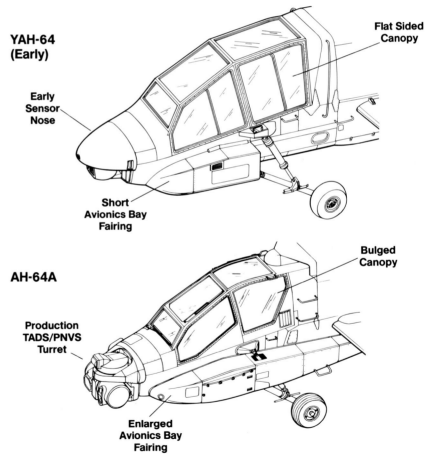

YAH-64 (Early)

Flat Sided Canopy

Early Sensor Nose

Short Avionics Bay Fairing

AH-64A

Bulged Canopy

Production TADS/PNVS Turret

Enlarged Avionics Bay Fairing

protect the crew. In the event of a crash, the crew is protected by roll bars that are built into the canopy frame. For fire protection, the Apache, is equipped with two self-sealing fuel cells which have a nitrogen inerting system that reduces the oxygen content in the fuel cells.

The Apache's two 1,723 shp General Electric T700-GE-701 turbo shaft engines can be started without outside assistance by use of the onboard 125 hp Garrett Air-Research Auxiliary Power Unit (APU). Engine exhaust is channeled though the McDonnell Douglas Black Hole infrared suppression system. The Black Hole system consists of a primary and three secondary cooling nozzles which reduce the temperature of the engine exhaust, thereby reducing the aircraft's IR signature. The primary nozzle draws in cool air and mixes it with the exhaust in the three secondary nozzles. The three secondary nozzles are installed at an outward angle to prevent a heat seeking missile from having direct view of the hot internal engine components.

The foldable four blades of the AH-64 main rotor system are attached to the main rotor head, which is linked directly to the drive shaft and supported by the static mast. The prototype's blades had the front half of the blade covered with stainless steel and the rear half covered in fiberglass. Production rotor blades are made of stainless steel tubes with a graphite composite overlay skinning. The tail rotor is of a scissors design with the blades set at 60° and 120° to each other. Thanks to the four blade main rotor and scissors tail rotor, the Apache has less than half the noise of earlier attack helicopters.

The landing gear is raked sharply back and consists of a Menasco trailing arm main landing gear with a fully castering self-centering and lockable tail wheel. The landing gear assembly is designed to absorb vertical impacts of up to 12 feet per second with no damage, and the main gear kneels for maintenance and air transportation aboard large Air Force transports.

Protection for the crew is of paramount importance in the Apache and is provided by the extensive use of lightweight Kevlar armor plating. Kevlar, made by DuPont, is both lightweight and ballistically resistant to small arms fire and shell splinters from larger cannon rounds (i.e. 23MM). A transparent armor glass blast shield separates the pilot from the copilot/gunner to prevent fragments from a hit in one cockpit from injuring both crew members. The pilot and copilot gunner sit in tandem under a tinted, glare resistant canopy that is not only crash worthy but also resistant to ground fire.

To further enhance crew survivability, the Apache is equipped with the Aircraft Survivability Equipment (ASE) system. The ASE system includes a passive radar warning receiver, an IR Jammer, a radar jammer, and a chaff/flare dispenser. The passive radar warning receiver can automatically engage the radar jammer if a threat radar is detected. The AN/ALQ-144 IR Jammer system is mounted on the upper fuselage immediately behind the rotor mast and generates pulsed IR energy to confuse the seeker head of IR guided missiles. The M130 chaff/flare dispenser, located on the left rear fuselage side, holds thirty M1 chaff rounds. Chaff or flares can be fired either automatically or manually if an incoming enemy missile attack is detected.

The Apache has phenomenal performance. It has a maximum level speed of 184 mph and a maximum design limit speed of 197 mph (although one prototype YAH-64 reached a dive speed of 237 mph during a structural test in 1980). The Apache has a range of 300 miles on internal fuel and a maximum ferry range (with external tanks) of 1,057 miles. Service ceiling is 21,000 feet and vertical rate of climb is 2,500 feet per minute.

Since going into production during 1983, the Apache has achieved a number of firsts. The AH-64 was the first production helicopter to launch laser guided munitions; the first to be equipped with a fly-by-wire-back-up flight control system; the first to incorporate ballistic protection against 23MM and 12.7MM weapons through the use of redundant flight and weapons systems and a structurally tolerant fuselage; the first to be compatible with a helmet mounted display which incorporates flight and weapons symbology and Forward Looking Infrared (FLIR) imagery; and the first to use a nitrogen inerted fuel system. Thus far, the Army has contracted for a total of 863 Apaches, with production expected to run well into the mid 1990s.

In June of 1989, Israel formally requested delivery of sixteen AH-64As under the

The Apache is assembled in the heart of Apache Indian territory at Mesa, Arizona. This early production AH-64A took part in the annual White Mountain Apache Indian Tribe's Labor Day festivities during 1984. (McDonnell Douglas)

A fully-armed Apache makes a low level, high speed pass causing the main rotor blades to bend upward. This upward flexing motion is known as coning. (U.S. Army photo by Frank Sullivan)

11

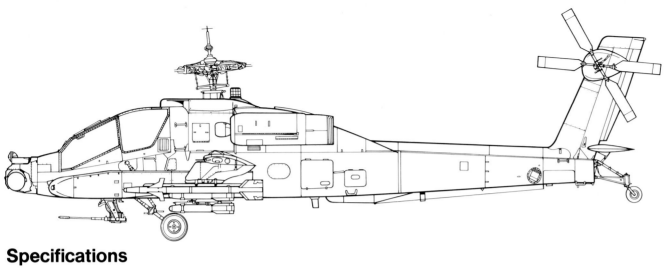

Specifications

AH-64A Apache

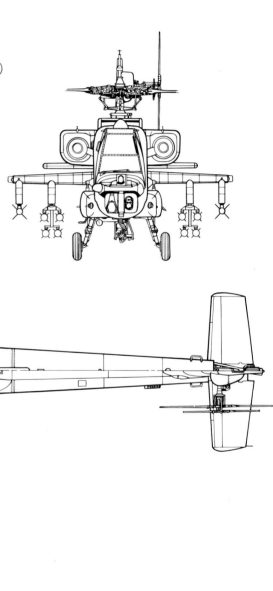

Rotor Diameter	48 feet
Length	57 feet 8 inches
Height	14 feet 1 inch
Empty Weight	10,760 pounds
Maximum Weight	21,000 pounds
Powerplants	Two 1,723 shp General Electric T700-GE-701 engines
Armament	One 30mm Chain Gun cannon, Hellfire anti-tank missiles, 2.75 inch rockets and AIM-9 Sidewinder air-to-air missiles.
Performance	
Maximum Speed	184 mph
Service ceiling	21,000 feet
Range	260 miles
Crew	Two

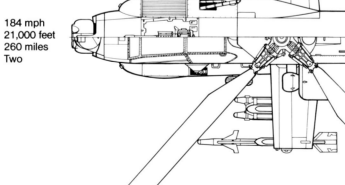

Foreign Military Sales Program. If approved, this will mark the first sale of the Apache to a foreign user. The Apaches are to be used by the Israeli Self Defense Force to augment the Bell AH-1S Cobra in the anti-armor role.

McDonnell Douglas and Westland Helicopters of England announced an agreement at the 1989 Paris Airshow for coproduction of the Apache in England if the AH-64 is selected by the British Army as its next attack helicopter. The British Army has a requirement for 125-150 such helicopters and a decision is expected during late 1989. Under the agreement, Westland will produce upwards of forty percent of the Apache airframe in England.

Negotiations are also currently ongoing toward possible sales of AH-64As to a number of other friendly nations. These negotiations are reportedly nearing finalization with Holland, while Japan, Korea, Egypt, and Spain have all expressed an interest in the Apache for use by their armed forces.

(Below) McDonnell Douglas Apaches are produced in a new facility constructed expressly for assembly of the AH-64A. These Apaches are being fitted with the main rotor system and other items of equipment as they move through the assembly area at Mesa. (McDonnell Douglas)

(Above) The prominent cheek sponsons on the Apache house electronics bays. The canopy is a mix of optically flat windshield and roof panels and curved side panels. The White rectangles on the wings, upper fuselage, and top of the tail are formation light luminescent panels. (McDonnell Douglas)

AH-64As are delivered to the Army painted in a Flat Dark Green camouflage scheme. The paint is a special type designed to partially absorb radar signals, reducing the enemy's ability to detect and track the Apache. The paint cannot be washed by conventional methods and is subject to uneven weathering. (Teledyne Ryan)

The AH-64A Apache is fully aerobatic and capable of performing a variety of maneuvers normally not preformed by helicopters including loops, rolls, split-Ss, and hammerhead stalls. There are no restrictions on the aircraft's maneuverability even when carrying a full weapons load. (McDonnell Douglas)

The bulge under the center fuselage of this AH-64A is the ADF antenna housing. Apaches are equipped with a wide variety of radios and navigational aids. One of the improvements planned for late production aircraft is the installation of an FM whip antenna which will be mounted on top of the vertical stabilizer. (U.S. Army)

Weapons Pylons

YAH-64

Tow Missile Launcher

Narrow Fixed Pylons

AH-64A

Hellfire Missile Launcher

Wide Movable Pylon

2.75 Inch Rocket Pod

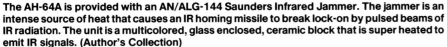

The AH-64A is provided with an AN/ALG-144 Saunders Infrared Jammer. The jammer is an intense source of heat that causes an IR homing missile to break lock-on by pulsed beams of IR radiation. The unit is a multicolored, glass enclosed, ceramic block that is super heated to emit IR signals. (Author's Collection)

This Apache is attached to the 145th Aviation Brigade at Fort Rucker, Alabama and is armed with eight Hellfire missiles, two 2.75 inch rocket pods and a 30 мм cannon. The nose sensor turret has been rotated to port and depressed to track a target below and left of the Apache. (U.S. Army by Frank Sullivan)

AH-64A Aircraft Survivability Equipment System

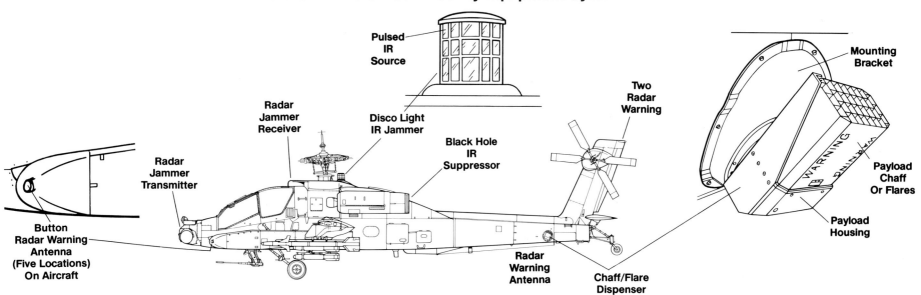

Pulsed IR Source

Disco Light IR Jammer

Radar Jammer Receiver

Two Radar Warning

Black Hole IR Suppressor

Mounting Bracket

Radar Jammer Transmitter

Payload Chaff Or Flares

Payload Housing

Button Radar Warning Antenna (Five Locations) On Aircraft

Radar Warning Antenna

Chaff/Flare Dispenser

Armament Systems

The Apache is armed with three separate weapons systems. For suppressive fire a 30MM chain gun is carried with 1,200 rounds of ammunition. For area suppressive fire, up to seventy-six 2.75 inch (70mm) Folding Fin Aerial Rockets (FFAR) can be carried, while the AH-64's primary anti-armor weapons system is the Hellfire laser guided missile.

All of the weapons sub-systems can be directed by either the pilot or copilot/gunner utilizing the Target Acquisition and Designation Sight/Forward Looking Infrared/Integrated Helmet and Display Sighting System. This combination of sighting systems makes the AH-64 a very formidable helicopter under any and all weather conditions.

The Apache's primary mission is anti-armor and for that mission it is armed with the Hellfire missile. Hellfire is an acronym standing for HELicopter Launched FIRE and forget. The missile is the primary point target weapon system on the Apache and can defeat armored or other hard targets. With an unclassified range of over 8 kilometers, the Hellfire can be fired from ground level at hover, or at maximum level flight speeds. The AGM-114 Hellfire can be employed using direct or indirect firing modes in single fire, rapid fire, or ripple fire engagements.

The Hellfire can be launched from sea level up to the Apache's maximum service ceiling (21,000 feet), and has a speed of Mach 1.7. The Hellfire, built by Rockwell International and Martin Marietta, is five feet four inches long and has a body diameter of seven inches. The Hellfire has two different motor options, either a mini-smoke rocket motor or an extended range pulsed rocket motor.

The heart of the missile system is its laser seeker system which almost guarantees a first round hit. The seeker homes on reflected laser light provided by the Apache, another airborne platform, or friendly ground troops. Although the laser seeker is currently the Hellfire's primary guidance system, there are two other versions of the missile under development. One uses imaging infrared (IIR), MilliMeter-wavelength radar (MM), or a Dual Mode (IIR/MM). These variants will give the flight crew the option of firing missiles in two different modes, lock on after launch (LOAL) or lock on before launch (LOBL).

The Hellfire missile launcher can be carried on each of the four under wing pylons of the Apache. The launcher itself is multifunctional and can accommodate either four Hellfire missiles per launcher, or (with slight modification) a combination of Stinger tube launched anti-aircraft missiles, Hellfires and/or 2.75 inch FFAR pods. The launcher can also be configured for either two or four Hellfire launch rails. The weapons pylons themselves are movable, which aids in aiming the various weapons carried on the pylon.

The M-230E-1, 30MM Chain Gun automatic cannon is the primary area suppressive fire weapon fitted to the Apache. The cannon also has the capability of destroying lightly armored vehicles such as the Soviet BMP at ranges out to 4,000 meters. Although not intended to be an air-to-air weapon, the cannon can be used against aerial targets such as enemy helicopters. The cannon is mounted in a hydraulically driven turret that can be traversed 110 ° left or right of the helicopter's centerline, it can be raised to 11 ° vertical and depressed to 60 °. In the event of loss of hydraulic power, the turret will lock in the current azimuth position and the gun will automatically return to the elevation up stowage position of 11 ° up.

The gun has a variable rate of fire from 600 to 650 rounds per minute and a muzzle velocity of 2,650 feet per second. The maximum capacity of the linkless ammunition storage system is 1,200 rounds. In normal operation the gun cycle is set at six 50 round bursts with five seconds between bursts, followed by a ten minute cooling period. Barrel life is projected to be some 10,000 rounds.

The most common type of ammunition carried is the M799 HEI (High Explosive Incendiary) or M789 HEDP (High Explosive Dual Purpose). This ammunition is interchangeable with British ADEN and French DEFA 30MM rounds utilized by NATO countries. The cannon is normally operated by the copilot/gunner using the Target Acquisition and Designation System (TADS), but may also be directed by either crew member using their helmet-mounted sighting systems.

Another area weapon carried by the Apache is the 2.75 inch (70MM) folding fin aerial rocket (FFAR). The rockets are housed in an LAU-3/A M-261 Hydra 70 launcher which has a nineteen round capacity. The 2.75 inch rockets have an effective range of 6,000 meters and can be fired from any altitude. There are many types of 2.75 inch rockets available, such as the M261 with a shaped charge warhead for use against armor or the M255 with a flechette warhead which contains over 2,500 one ounce steel flechettes (darts) for use against enemy ground troops and soft skin vehicles.

The U.S. Army is currently examining other missile systems for compatibility with the Apache. These systems include: the Stinger, Sidewinder, and Mistral air-to-air missiles; the Harpoon and Penguin anti-ship missiles; the AGM-122A Sidearm anti-radiation missile, and TOW tube launched anti-tank missiles. Thus far, the Stinger and Sidewinder have been cleared for use with the Apache, with the Mistral nearing completion of its testing. The Harpoon and Penguin are intended for the naval variant, which is still in the development stage. Early Apaches had the provision for use of the TOW, and this weapons system is cleared for use; however, at this time it is intended solely for use on a possible Apache variant intended for the U.S. Marine Corps (and possible export customers not cleared for Hellfire technology).

This Apache is conducting live fire tests of the Hellfire anti-tank missile. For the tests the Hellfires are painted Red and White to make it easier for recording cameras to track them. Currently the Hellfire has two guidance systems available, laser or IR (Infrared). The modular construction of the Hellfire makes it easy to change seekers in the field. (McDonnell Douglas)

This Hellfire is about to score a direct hit on a target tank hull. The AGM-114 Hellfire was guided to the target by reflected laser light which can be directed on the target from either the AH-64, another aircraft or a ground team. (Rockwell)

An AH-64 Apache moves in to take a close look at the damage done to a target tank at the Yuma Proving Grounds. The primary mission of the AH-64 is anti-armor, and to perform this mission the Apache is armed with a 30mm cannon, 2.75 inch (FFAR) rockets, and Hellfire anti-tank missiles. (U.S. Army)

Operational Hellfires are delivered painted in Dark Green with U.S. Army in Yellow on the missile's sides. Hellfires can be equipped with two different rocket motors; either a mini-smoke motor or an extended range pulsed rocket motor. (Rockwell)

The Sidewinder currently has been cleared for use by the Apache, with the missile and launcher rail being mounted on either outboard weapons pylon. An alternative wing tip launcher is under development, which would allow the Apache to carry two AIM-9L Sidewinders without losing the use of its underwing pylons for anti-armor weapons. The Army views the Sidewinder as an interim weapon, intended to give the Apache an air-to-air self defense capability while development of the Stinger air-to-air system is finalized.

The Stinger tube-launched air-to-air missile system has been selected to be the primary air-to-air self defense weapon carried by the Apache (although the Hellfire can be used in an emergency). An air-launched version of the man-portable, tube-launched Stinger missile system has been successfully developed and current planning calls for two such weapons to be carried on wing tip launchers, giving the Apache a total of four Stingers. By mounting the missile tubes on the wing tips, they do not interfere with the Apache's primary anti-armor missile load. Installation of the air-to-air Stinger (ATAS) on the AH-64A is expected to begin during late 1989.

Also compatible with the Stinger launch system is the French Mistral tube launched air-to-air missile which has the performance and other properties that are very similar to those of the Stinger. The ability to use these missiles enhances NATO commonality for Apache units operating in Europe.

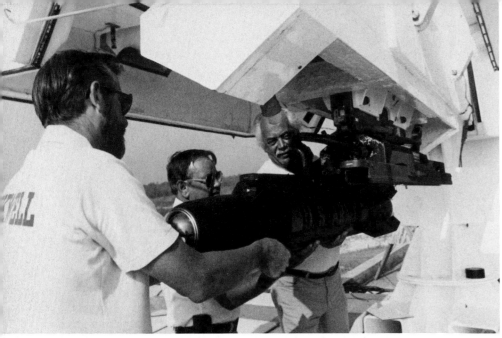

Rockwell employees install a production Hellfire onto a modular launcher rail on a test hardstand at Eglin Air Force Base, Florida, where initial test firings of the Hellfire took place. The test hardstands are designed to handle the wide variety of missile types tested at Eglin. (Rockwell)

An AH-64A Apache launches a Hellfire anti-tank missile at the Army's Yuma, Arizona test range. The live fire exercise, conducted by members of the 1st Squadron, 6th Cavalry Regiment (Air Combat), was the first such exercise conducted by an operational Apache unit. This Apache is equipped with a Disco Light IR jammer behind the rotor mast. (McDonnell Douglas)

The stub wing pylon of an AH-64A armed with four Hellfire missiles and two Hydra 70 (LAU 61 A/A) 2.75 inch rocket launchers. The 2.75 inch rocket launcher weighs seventy-nine pounds empty and has a capacity of nineteen 2.75 inch folding fin aerial rockets (FFAR). (Author's collection)

Hellfire Modular Missile Launcher

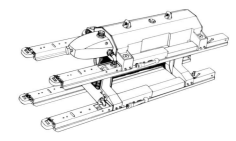

18

The AH-64A is equipped with a 30MM M230 Chain Gun mounted under the forward fuselage. The cannon is the primary suppressive fire weapon for use against both ground or air targets. The weapon has a variable firing rate of 600 or 650 rounds per minute and a maximum effective range of 4,000 meters. (Author's Collection)

An Apache cannon silhouettes another AH-64A Apache of the 6th Cavalry at Fort Hood, Texas. Fort Hood is called Apache Town USA and is the home of the Army's Apache training program that provides combat ready crews for other units around the country and for service in Europe. (McDonnell Douglas)

This armorer is securing the loadhead assembly and loading adapter to the cannon round accepter/ejection flange. The cannon can use American made M789 High Explosive Dual Purpose (HEDP) and M799 High Explosive Incendiary (HEI) rounds or ADEN/DEFA ammunition used by NATO forces. (U.S. Army)

This armorer of the 6th Cavalry is inspecting the 30MM rounds before they are loaded into the loading adapter. During ground servicing, ground crews wear ear protection to protect them from the noise of the equipment. The ammunition being loaded is M788 Practice rounds, which are painted with a Blue band for identification. (U.S. Army)

19

An AH-64A is enveloped in a shower of fire as it launches a salvo of 2.75 inch FFAR rockets during a live fire exercise on the Fort Rucker, Alabama firing range. The circular object just behind the rotor mast is the Disco Light IR Jammer. (U.S. Army)

This AH-64A is firing rockets from a hover. Crews report that the Apache is a very effective and steady platform for launching rockets. The smoke cloud ahead of the Apache is from one of the rockets. (McDonnell Douglas)

Army armorers load the port outer rocket pod of an Apache with 2.75 inch folding fin rockets. The AH-64A can carry up to seventy-six of these rockets in four nineteen shot underwing pods. The rockets have an effective range of 6,000 meters and can be fitted with a variety of warheads. (U.S. Army)

Hydra 70 2.75 Inch Rocket Pods

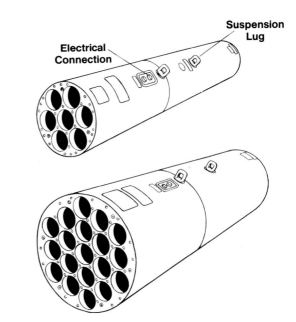

The AIM-9 Sidewinder was first fired from an AH-64A during 1988 at the Yuma, Arizona, test range. The AIM-9L Sidewinder, carried by the AH-64, features all aspect acquisition and intercept capabilities against all types of aerial targets. (McDonnell Douglas)

This AH-64A is armed with both Stinger and Sidewinder air-to-air missiles. The AIM-9 Sidewinder was mounted on the starboard outboard pylon and a pair of Stinger launcher tubes were mounted on the port outer pylon. Currently, the Army is planning to mount Stingers on special wing tip mounts and leave the underwing pylons for air-to-ground weapons. (McDonnell Douglas)

Sidewinder Missile Installation

AH-64A

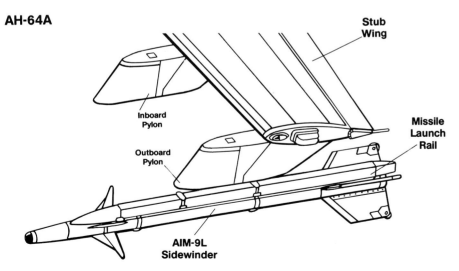

Stub Wing

Inboard Pylon

Outboard Pylon

Missile Launch Rail

AIM-9L Sidewinder

This Apache is conducting an acceptance flight near the McDonnell Douglas facility at Mesa, Arizona. The desert around Mesa is quite similar to the terrain found in the Middle East. If ongoing negotiations with Israel prove successful, Apaches may soon be operating over the deserts of the Middle East. (McDonnell Douglas)

Optional Weapons

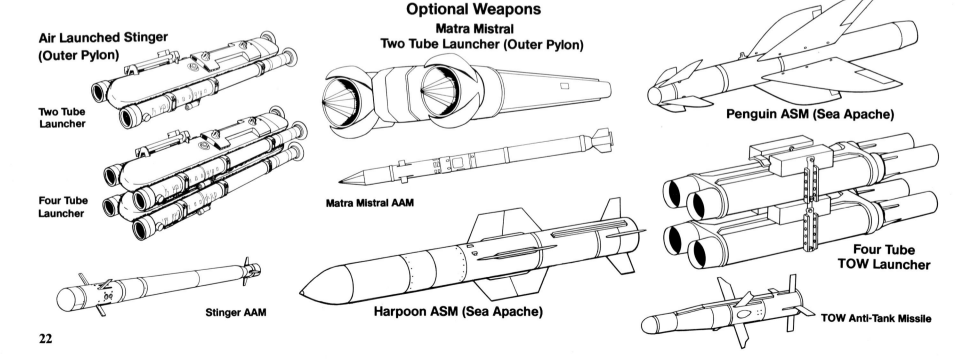

Air Launched Stinger
(Outer Pylon)

Two Tube
Launcher

Four Tube
Launcher

Stinger AAM

Matra Mistral
Two Tube Launcher (Outer Pylon)

Matra Mistral AAM

Harpoon ASM (Sea Apache)

Penguin ASM (Sea Apache)

Four Tube
TOW Launcher

TOW Anti-Tank Missile

Visionics and Avionics

The Apache's integrated weapons, electronic, and visionic (combined visual and electronic) system, is the most modern of any helicopter in the world. Housed in the nose turret of the Apache are the two primary sensor systems, the Target Acquisition Designator System (TADS) and the Pilot's Night Vision Sensor system (PNVS). The TADS contains high power direct-view optics, a Forward Looking Infrared (FLIR) sensor for night operations, a high resolution television system for day operations, a laser target designator/range finder and a laser spot tracker. Fire control data collected by the TADS is fed through the on-board computer to the crew for weapons selection and firing.

The PNVS is mounted on top of the TADS turret and is capable of 90° horizontal movement right and left of the helicopter centerline and a plus 20°/minus 45° vertical movement. The TADS has a horizontal movement of 120° right or left of centerline and plus 30°/minus 60° vertical movement. Normally the TADS is operated by the copilot/gunner; however, the video display may be utilized by either crew member. The wide field of view FLIR also provides a back up capability for the PNVS.

The AN/AAQ-11 PNVS provides the pilot (through the Integrated Helmet and Display Sight, IHADSS) with real time thermal imagery of the surrounding terrain. This permits combat operations during adverse weather and in total darkness. The pilot is continuously provided with high resolution imagery and full flight/weapons symbology by the monocle that is placed in front of his right eye. The nose turret also houses the radar jammer transmitter antenna which is mounted on the TADS support structure. The receiver antenna for the radar jammer is located on the upper cabin area just forward of the rotor mast.

Avionics and navigation equipment aboard the Apache is state-of-the-art and extensive. Air-to-air and air-to-ground communications is handled by secure voice UHF-AM, VHF-AM, and FM radios. To aid in navigation, the Apache crew is provided with an Automatic Directional Finder (ADF) and a Lightweight Doppler Navigational System (LDNS). The LDNS provides the pilot with his present position or destination navigation information displayed in either latitude and longitude or universal mercator coordinates. The system also has a radar absolute altimeter which produces extremely accurate altitude indications from 0 to 1,500 feet. Another of the navigational aids installed in the Apache is the Heading Altitude Reference System (HARS) that not only permits accurate nap-of-the-earth flying but also provides for storage of target location data during an overfly. The avionics equipment also includes an Identification Friend or Foe (IFF) transponder that transmits a specially coded reply to a ground or air based IFF radar interrogator system.

One of the most prominent features of the Apache is the Air Data Sensor (ADS) located on top of the rotor mast. This sensing instrument provides ambient pressure and temperature; air density ratio; vertical, longitudinal and lateral airspeed; and angle of side slip. The information is fed through the on board computer and is used to compute fire control solutions and provide inputs for the Digital Automatic Stabilization Equipment (DASE). The DASE uses the information from the ADS and the HARS to aid the pilot with automatic control inputs. The DASE permits the Apache to achieve a rate of roll of 130 degrees per second at speeds between 120 and 140 knots, making it one of the most maneuverable helicopters in the world.

Each crew member is provided with his own instrument panel, optimized for his particular role. The pilot is provided with a full range of instruments ranging from older analog types, to vertical scale instruments and a video display unit (VDU). The analog equipment includes: an airspeed indicator, barometric and absolute altimeters, and an instantaneous vertical speed indicator (IVSI). The vertical scale type instruments include: gauges for fuel quantity, engine torque, engine oil pressure, and engine gas temperature

among others. The Video Display Unit (VDU) provides the pilot with necessary flight information along with navigational data, and weapons data such as the missile lock on constraint window. The VDU also portrays accurate terrain imagery provided by the FLIR and PNVS.

The copilot/gunner's panel has only basic analog flight instruments such as an airspeed indicator, barometric altimeter, and remote altitude indicator. Engine data is restricted to an engine/rotor speed gauge and engine torque indicator. The heart of the copilot/gunner's instrument panel is the weapons system control panel. The multipurpose sight system is in the center of the panel and contains the TADS, FLIR, weapons controls, Fault Detection/Location system, and controls for the Optical Relay Tube (ORT). The ORT and associated hand controls and switches provide weapon symbology, guidance, and flight altitudes. The system is capable of target tracking using a combination of TV, IR, and laser under any type of weather conditions, twenty-four hours a day.

Early Apache critics had stated that the sensor system, especially the FLIR, could easily be fooled when operating in the rain and drizzle of Western Europe. Under these conditions targets would be obscured by the rain and their IR signature reduced. During the Apache's first deployment and exercise in Europe the system proved that it could detect, track, and attack targets under all weather conditions. In operations against the British, Apache crews scored kills under conditions of rain, fog, and smoke. Often the British crews refused to believe that they had been attacked (they had never seen the Apache) until they were shown video pictures of their vehicle clearly outlined in the cross hairs of the attacking Apache.

The TADS/PNVS turret is assembled at the Martin-Marietta Electronics Plant in Orlando, Florida. The TADS section of the turret contains high power direct view optics, a Forward Looking Infrared (FLIR) sensor for night operations, a high resolution television system for day operations and a laser target designator/range finder. (Martin Marietta)

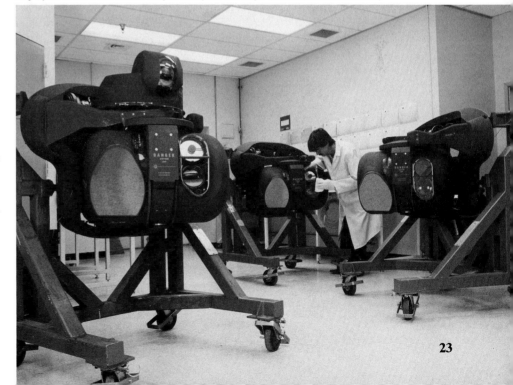

The nose of the AH-64A houses the TADS/PNVS turret. TADS is an acronym for Target Acquisition Designator System, while PNVS stands for Pilot's Night Vision Sensor. The TADS occupies the lower section of the turret while the PNVS is mounted above it. (Martin Marietta)

(Above) The TADS turret can rotate 120 ° either right or left of the aircraft centerline and has a vertical range of motion of plus 30 ° and minus 60 °. The PNVS turret, above the TADS unit, can scan through 90 ° right or left of the centerline and plus 20 °/minus 45 ° in the vertical mode. (Author's Collection)

(Left) The optics of the TADS/PNVS turret are protected while on the ground by special plastic covers. These covers protect the lens from being scratched, chipped, or damaged by foreign objects. The bulge on the port fuselage is a rear view mirror and the small circular antenna on the sponson is a radar warning receiver antenna. (Author's Collection)

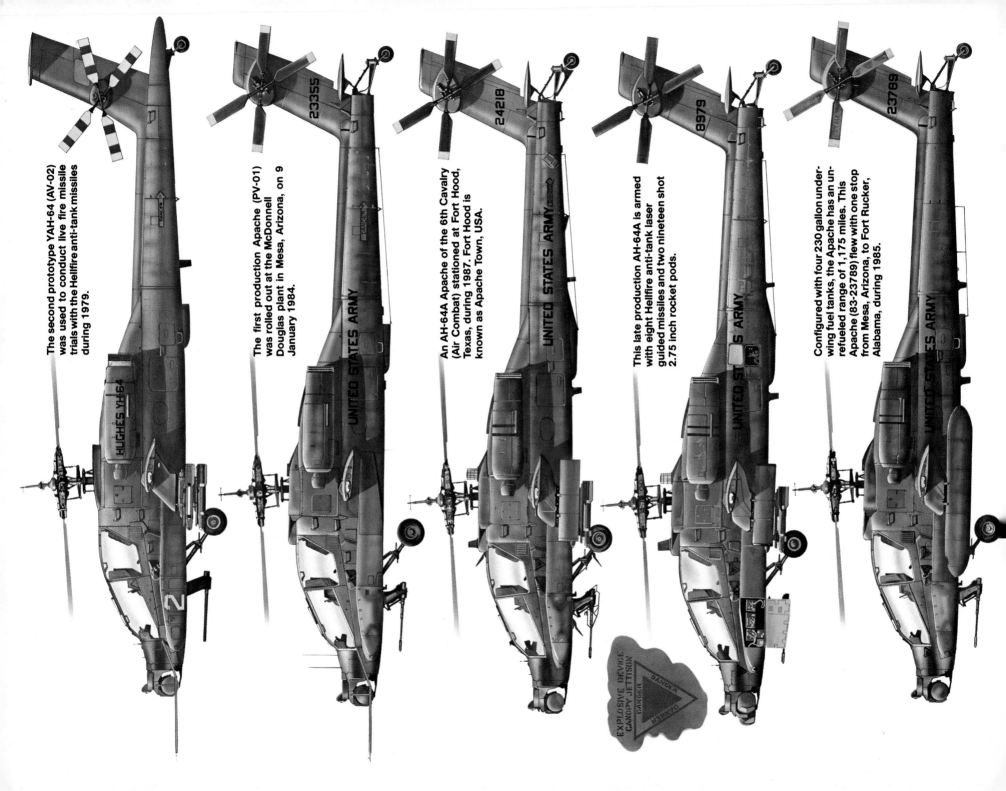

The second prototype YAH-64 (AV-02) was used to conduct live fire missile trials with the Hellfire anti-tank missiles during 1979.

The first production Apache (PV-01) was rolled out at the McDonnell Douglas plant in Mesa, Arizona, on 9 January 1984.

An AH-64A Apache of the 6th Cavalry (Air Combat) stationed at Fort Hood, Texas, during 1987. Fort Hood is known as Apache Town, USA.

This late production AH-64A is armed with eight Hellfire anti-tank laser guided missiles and two nineteen shot 2.75 inch rocket pods.

Configured with four 230 gallon under-wing fuel tanks, the Apache has an un-refueled range of 1,175 miles. This Apache (83-23789) flew with one stop from Mesa, Arizona, to Fort Rucker, Alabama, during 1985.

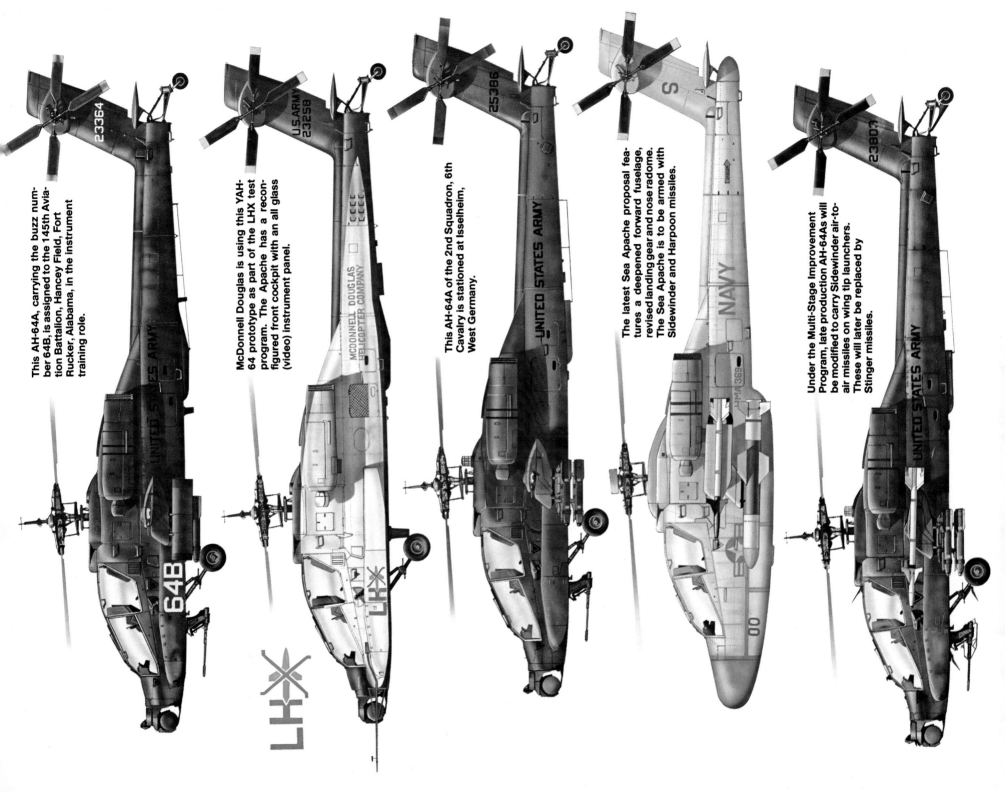

This AH-64A, carrying the buzz number 64B, is assigned to the 145th Aviation Battalion, Hancey Field, Fort Rucker, Alabama, in the instrument training role.

McDonnell Douglas is using this YAH-64 prototype as part of the LHX test program. The Apache has a reconfigured front cockpit with an all glass (video) instrument panel.

This AH-64A of the 2nd Squadron, 6th Cavalry is stationed at Isselheim, West Germany.

The latest Sea Apache proposal features a deepened forward fuselage, revised landing gear and nose radome. The Sea Apache is to be armed with Sidewinder and Harpoon missiles.

Under the Multi-Stage Improvement Program, late production AH-64As will be modified to carry Sidewinder air-to-air missiles on wing tip launchers. These will later be replaced by Stinger missiles.

(Above) An early style Air Data Sensor (ADS) probe was installed on the prototype YAH-64 and combined the functions of both the ADS sensor and that of a test instrument probe. It replaced the test probe that had been mounted on the prototype's nose. (Author's Collection)

(Right) The production version of the Air Data Sensor (ADS) mounted on the rotor mast of the AH-64A provides information such as air density, longitudinal and lateral airspeed to the Digital Automatic Stabilization Equipment (DASE) and fire control computer. (Author's Collection)

The pilot's instrument panel of the AH-64A is equipped with a full range of analog and digital instruments along with a video display unit (VDU) in the panel center. The VDU displays altitude, speed, attitude, and weapons control and status information. A transparent blast shield is between the pilot and copilot/gunner to protect them from shell fragments. (McDonnell Douglas)

The copilot/gunner's cockpit of the AH-64 is dominated by the multi-purpose sight system in the center of the instrument panel. The sight system contains an optical relay tube and handgrips with small circular "coolie hat" switches. The copilot/gunner can operate the complete weapons system with this sight. (McDonnell Douglas)

Both pilot and copilot/gunner are provided with Helmet Display Units (HDU) that, when placed in front of the right eye, display selected video and/or symbology to each crew member. The HDU consists of a one inch cathrode ray tube mounted in a high impact plastic barrel. (Martin Marietta)

The TADS/PNVS turret and 30мм cannon can be slaved to the movements of either the pilot or copilot/gunner by a pair of Sensor Surveying Units (SSU) that are placed on the upper arm wings of each crew member's seat. The SSU generates IR beams that sweep the crew stations and feed position data to the Sight Electronics Unit (SEU). (McDonnell Douglas)

Armored Crew Seat

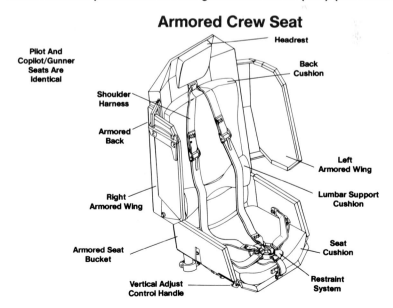

Pilot And Copilot/Gunner Seats Are Identical

Headrest

Back Cushion

Shoulder Harness

Armored Back

Left Armored Wing

Lumbar Support Cushion

Right Armored Wing

Armored Seat Bucket

Seat Cushion

Vertical Adjust Control Handle

Restraint System

Into Service

Training

Since 1954, the Army has trained both its fixed and rotary wing pilots at Fort Rucker, Alabama. Student pilots enter an intensive flying program that can take up to a year to complete, at a cost of one million dollars per pilot. When his training is complete, the new Army pilot joins one of the best and most dedicated group of men and women aviators in the world.

After a pilot wins his wings, his training continues with both actual flying and a large amount of simulator training. Perhaps the most innovative and cost effective training takes place in the simulator. Simulators, like the aircraft that they represent, have evolved dramatically. The Link Company, a division of Singer, has built simulators since before the Second World War. Early Link Trainers were used by all services to train student aviators in the fine art of instrument flying without ever leaving the ground.

Today's generation simulators are an exact replica of the cockpit, flying controls, and instruments of the an actual aircraft. These simulators produce motion, vibration, sound, and visual effects that give the student a real feeling of flight. The Apache Combat Mission Simulator (CMS), built by Link-Singer, puts the pilot and copilot/gunner in

Since the pilot and copilot/gunner have different functions and instrument panels in the AH-64, much of their training is conducted in separate but linked Apache Combat Mission Simulators (CMS). The Singer-Link simulators have the feel of flight in the actual aircraft without the associated costs. (Singer-Link)

separate simulators that move in concert with each other. The theme of the CMS mission profile is "kill or be killed" as the instructor runs the crew through a simulated combat mission. To vary the training, the instructor has up to fifteen preprogrammed threat scenarios available to him.

The CMS can freely move through sixty degrees of motion giving it the capability to conduct rather violent maneuvers. The CMS can also simulate situations that you would not want to perform in an actual aircraft, such as engine outages, battle damage, and fire.

The use of the simulator saves the Army a great deal of money. Operating costs for an Apache is $1,820.00 per hour, where as the simulator can be operated for only $625.00 per hour. The real savings are readily apparent in weapons training. 30MM cannon rounds cost $10.49 each, 2.75 inch FFARs costs $199.00 per rocket, and each Hellfire missile costs $26,000.00. In the CMS all these weapons can be simulated for a fraction of their costs.

The Apache CMS at Fort Rucker is kept in operation sixteen hours a day, seven days a week, with maintenance begin performed at night. There are three Apache Combat Mission Simulators, one at Fort Rucker, one at Fort Hood, Texas and the third at Isselheim West Germany. Four additional simulators are due to be deployed in the near future.

An interesting feature of the AH-64 simulator is that it can be linked to other simulators such as the AH-1 Cobra, OH-58 Scout, CH-47 Chinook and UH-60 Blackhawk simulators for combined arms team exercises. The realism of simulator flying was highlighted by SGT Ben Goneberg, who stated that, "a student aviator proficient in the UH-1 Huey can transition to the Apache right in the simulator after only a few hours training."

The Army estimates that the Apache simulator saves the American taxpayers at least seven million dollars a year and turns out a better trained Army aviator in the process.

Operations

In February of 1986, the 6th Cavalry Brigade (Air Combat) began receiving their first AH-64A assigning them to its 3rd Squadron stationed at Fort Hood, Texas. The 3rd Squadron was responsible for evaluating the Apache under field conditions as part of the Army Readiness Training and Evaluation Program (ARTEP) and for establishing the Apache certification course for all Apache crewmen.

The 3rd became the first Apache unit to be fully certified by ARTEP and declared combat ready. The 3rd was soon joined at Fort Hood, which has become known as Apache Town USA, by the 1st and 2nd Squadrons which rapidly completed training and were certified ready. This training was soon to pay off when the 1st and 3rd Squadrons were slated to take part in Exercise *Certain Strike '87* one of the *Reforger* (return of forces to Germany) series of exercises.

Upon completion of *Certain Strike '87* the 2nd Squadron was permanently stationed at Isselheim, West Germany as part of the VII Corps Aviation Brigade. Besides its eighteen AH-64As, the 2nd also has three UH-60A Blackhawk helicopters for the utility mission and thirteen OH-58D scout helicopters. The OH-58D and AH-64s operate as hunter-killer teams with the OH-58s being used to scout ahead of the Apache force, locating targets for the Apaches.

Other units being equipped with the Apache are the 17th Cavalry, 2nd Armored Division and certain units from the 3rd Armored Division in Germany. When these units have completed certification through the ARTEP at Fort Hood, a total of over 200 Apaches will be stationed with various cavalry and armored units in West Germany alone.

With the operational deployment of the Apache to Europe, it is inevitable that the AH-64 Apache will be compared to the Soviet Mi 24 Hind F, although the two aircraft were designed to meet completely different requirements. The Hind weighs 24,250 pounds in its standard mission configuration compared to 14,445 pounds for the Apache. This weight difference does not have an impact on speed (both the Hind and Apache have maximum cruise speeds in the 180 mph range) but the additional weight of the Hind directly impacts on operational combat range. The Hind has a range of under 100 miles, while the lighter Apache has a range of 280 miles. One unique advantage of the Hind is its ability to carry eight combat equipped troops plus the crew of three. The Apache has no such capability because it was designed solely as a two seat tank killer.

The Apache has a distinct advantage in its electronic, avionic and visionic suite. The Soviet Bloc countries have lagged behind the US in their development of sophisticated electronics technology, usually by some five or more years. Where the Soviets have always believed in the premise of quantity is better than quality, the US has always relied on and subscribed to quality as the way to even the superior Soviet numbers.

The U.S. Army National Guard began receiving the AH-64A during 1987, with the 1st Battalion, 130th Attack Helicopter Regiment of the North Carolina National Guard, stationed at Raleigh-Durham Airport, North Carolina, being the first to convert to the Apache. Two other Guard Apache units have completed transition, the 1st Battalion, 151st Aviation Regiment, 18th Airborne Corps of the South Carolina National Guard, and the 111th Aviation Regiment, Flordia National Guard, while a fourth unit, assigned to the Utah National Guard has begun training key personnel. It is expected that between 1988 and 1990 the Army National Guard will re-equip over fifteen battalions with the Apache.

Faced with shrinking budgets, the Army has had to scale back Apache procurement. Currently there are contracts covering a total of 675 AH-64As. This figure is far short of the 1,031 that the Army requires to replace the AH-1 Cobras that remain in the Army inventory. Long range Army goals call for a total of forty-seven Apache battalions, each with fifteen to eighteen AH-64s. This plan, like all military procurement plans, is subject to the approval of the budget planners in Congress. These planners would do well to remember that as of 1987, the Warsaw Pact armies enjoyed a two to one advantage in main battle tanks over the NATO forces, with a total of some 56,000 tanks.

World Wide Deployment

The Apache is capable of being deployed over great distances to an area of potential combat operations in three ways. It can self-deploy, be shipped by sea, or air deployed aboard large USAF transport aircraft. Self-deployment is accomplished by using four 230 gallon extended range underwing fuel tanks. Configured with four tanks the Apache's range is increased to 1,175 miles, with a twenty minute reserve. This means that a flight of Apaches can depart from the US and fly directly to Europe, although this is not the quickest way to deploy overseas.

The fastest method (and easiest on the Apache pilots) is to deploy by Air Force transport aircraft. A total of six Apaches can be loaded on board a C-5A transport, while the C-141B can carry two, and a C-130 can carry one. It takes seven Army mechanics one hour per aircraft to prepare and load six Apaches for air shipment on a C-5.

During 1985, the first long range validation test flight for the Apache took place under the test designation, Apache Long Legs. The flight was planned to go from Mesa, Arizona to Fort Rucker, Alabama using four 230 gallon underwing fuel tanks. These fuel tanks are constructed of lightweight Kevlar, the same material used as armor plate in the AH-64. With the tanks fitted and topped off, the Apache grosses out at over 21,000

pounds, well over its primary mission weight of 14,445 pounds.

During 1986 two Apaches were sent via sea shipment to Germany for a demonstration tour. One of the purposes of this trip was to validate the Army's procedures of shipping the Apache via ship or barge. The tour also was a test in preparation for Exercise *Certain Strike '87*, the 19th *Reforger* (return of forces to Germany) exercise. Forty Apaches from the 1st and 2nd Squadrons, 6th Cavalry Brigade (Air Combat) deployed to Germany by ship as part the exercise. Once the exercise was completed the 2nd Squadron was permanently stationed at Isselheim, Germany.

This copilot/gunner is practicing a weapons delivery with the TADS sight in the simulator. When the gunner is in this head down position, TADS operation is controlled by the manual track switch on the right hand grip, and weapons firing is controlled with the switches located on the left hand grip. (Singer-Link)

Training of U.S. Army aviators takes place at Fort Rucker, Alabama, and at various stage fields in the vicinity. These army aviators have just landed at Eck Army Air Field, one of the stage fields at Fort Rucker, and are about to report to the operations shack. The AH-64A in the background has a side number (19K) that uses the last two digits of the serial number (85-23819). (Author's Collection)

This AH-64A (82-23364) is undergoing preflight inspection parked on the Fort Rucker Army Aviation Center (AAC) ramp. The serial number on the fin and fuselage identification number (64B) are in White. The painted section of the ramp is a reproduction of the Fort Rucker AAC patch. (U.S. Army)

This AH-64A (85-24265) at Eck Army Air Field carries the buzz number (65E) on the fuselage side in White. The Apache is configured as an instrument trainer and is based at Fort Rucker, Alabama. Contrary to standard Army practices, Apaches carry no Orange trainer panels to identify them as instrument trainers. (Author's Collection)

Eck Army Airfield is used as a stage field for AH-64 training. The field is used primarily for practice landings and takeoffs, instrument approaches and other flight training associated with the Apache program. The TADS/PNVS turret on the Apache in the foreground has been rotated to the stowed position. (Author's Collection)

Army ground crews perform maintenance on the rotor hub of an AH-64A at Fort Rucker. The engine access panels are stressed to also serve as maintenance stands. Maintenance is further eased by the fact that most electronic components can be worked on from ground level. (U.S. Army)

An Army aviator prepares to man his AH-64A at Eck Army Air Field, Alabama. Both pilot and copilot/gunner enter the aircraft through the opening canopy panels on the starboard side. During Apache training, flight time is interspersed with time in the Combat Mission Simulator (CMS). (Author's Collection)

Ground maintenance personnel inspect the engines, rotor system, instruments and armament systems on this AH-64A (buzz number 40) inside one of the maintenance hangars at Fort Rucker. Later the buzz number will have a letter code added to it. (U.S. Army)

This AH-64A (40) is undergoing periodic maintenance inspection in one of the hangars at Fort Rucker. The Apache was designed to operate with the troops in the field, and most major mechanical and electronic components are modular to ease maintenance and reduce the time the aircraft is down for repairs. (U.S. Army)

33

An AH-64A (85-23789) takes off on a practice long-range flight fitted with four 230 gallon underwing fuel tanks. The 230 gallon tanks are made of Kevlar, the same lightweight armor material that is used to protect the crew and other vulnerable areas of the AH-64. (McDonnell Douglas)

When configured with external fuel tanks, the Apache has an unrefueled range of 1,175 miles and can self-deploy to most of the hot spots around the world. With the four 230 gallon tanks in place, the AH-64 has a gross weight of over 21,000 pounds. (McDonnell Douglas)

The test AH-64A touches down at Fort Rucker, Alabama at the end of the long range validation flight from Mesa, Arizona. The flight was made with only one stop, thanks to the added range afforded by the four 230 gallon long range tanks. For extended range search and destroy missions, two tanks and Hellfire or other missile systems could be fitted. (U.S. Army)

Before the AH-64 can be loaded onto a transport aircraft, the main rotor blades must be stowed or removed and tail rotors removed. The weapon pylons and wings are folded and in some instances the cannon must be removed as well. Once the AH-64 reaches its destination, the removed and/or stored items are repositioned and the Apache is combat ready. (McDonnell Douglas.)

AH-64A Tow Bar

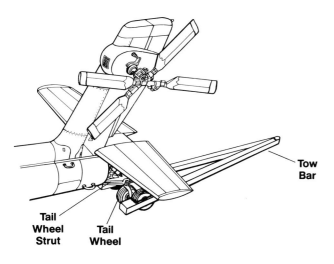

Tow
Bar

Tail
Wheel
Strut

Tail
Wheel

The quickest way to deploy an AH-64 squadron is to load them aboard USAF transports such as the giant Lockheed C-5. The C-5 can load six Apaches, taking one hour per Apache. Most of this time is taken up by securing the lashings and positioning the helicopters in the C-5. (McDonnell Douglas)

An AH-64 is being loaded aboard a Lockheed C-5 Transport, which has a capacity of six AH-64s. The Lockheed C-141 can handle two, a Lockheed C-130 can carry one, while the new McDonnell Douglas C-17 can transport three. (McDonnell Douglas)

35

The flight crew of this Apache (84-24218) conduct a pre-flight inspection at one of Fort Hood's remote fields. During field deployments, the air crew wear Kevlar helmets until they board the Apache. Once on board, their Kevlar helmets are stowed in the aft stowage bay. (McDonnell Douglas)

A pair of fully armed Apaches take off from a grass field on an early morning training mission near Fort Hood, Texas. Both aircraft are equipped with the Disco Light infrared (IR) jammer unit behind the main rotor masts. (McDonnell Douglas)

A flight of AH-64As over the German country side during Exercise *Certain Strike '87*, one of the Reforger (return of forces to Germany) series of exercises. The 1st and 2nd Squadron of the 6th Cavalry (Air Combat) took part in the exercise deploying with over thirty AH-64A Apaches. (McDonnell Douglas)

The AH-64A began active service with the 6th Cavalry Brigade (Air Combat) during 1986, when the 3rd Squadron became certified by the ARTEP at Fort Hood, Texas. Normally AH-64As carry no unit markings and the serial numbers and all external markings (with the exception of the Red tail rotor warning) are in Flat Black. (U.S. Army)

The Apache is routinely flown at night (and in bad weather) using the Pilot's Night Vision Sensor (PNVS) for navigation. Apaches usually work in hunter-killer teams with either another Apache or an OH-58 Kiowa scout helicopter. (McDonnell Douglas)

Air and ground crewmen go over an Apache mission plan at Fort Hood, Texas. These Apaches are assigned to the 6th Cavalry Brigade, the only separate air cavalry unit currently on strength with the U.S. Army. (McDonnell Douglas)

Pilot's Night Vision Sensor

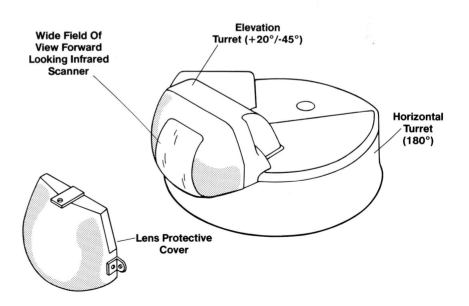

Wide Field Of View Forward Looking Infrared Scanner

Elevation Turret (+20°/-45°)

Horizontal Turret (180°)

Lens Protective Cover

This AH-64A is assigned to the 130th Attack Helicopter Battalion, North Carolina National Guard. Besides North Carolina, other Guard units currently equipped with the Apache are the 151st Aviation Regiment, South Carolina National Guard and the 111th Aviation Regiment, Florida National Guard. By 1990 the Guard will have fifteen Apache Battalions. (McDonnell Douglas)

An AH-64A Apache makes a landing at a forward rearming area under the direction of a ground crewman. Rockets and Hellfire missile containers are visible just ahead of the Apache. In combat, the Apache would use such areas to rapidly reload and return to action. Once the missiles are loaded they are given a go/no-go test from the cockpit, and the Apache is once again combat ready. (U.S. Army)

Ground crewmen load ammunition into the magazine of an AH-64A (85-25386) using the uploading adapter. Rather than removing the 1,200 round magazine from the aircraft to reload it, the adapter allows the ground crew to feed rounds directly into the ammunition feed system. The adapter can be used to either load or down-load ammunition. (Western Design)

Most minor maintenance can be accomplished in the field from ground level. This crewman is working in the forward avionics/electronics bay which contains components of the fire control system. The Apache has miles of wiring connecting the various electronic systems and sub-systems. (U.S. Army)

(Above) Ground crewmen load 2.75 inch FFAR rockets into the port rocket launcher of an AH-64A. The crewmen wear radio headsets to communicate with the aircrew and for noise protection. These rockets have Blue warheads to signify that they are practice rounds. (U.S. Army)

(Left) An Apache of the 6th Cavalry hovers behind the tree line in a German forest. *Certain Strike '87* was designed to show the deployability and quick reaction time of the 6th Cavalry in a combat situation. On completion of the exercise, the 2nd Squadron was permanently assigned to the VII Corps Aviation Brigade, at Isselheim, West Germany. (McDonnell Douglas)

Sea Apache

Studies for a Naval version of the Apache were begun during 1984 and since that time the McDonnell Douglas Helicopter Company has proposed several navalized Apaches to both the U.S. Marine Corps and U.S. Navy. The navalized Apache is viewed as a replacement for the aging Bell AH-1 Sea Cobras that are in service with the Navy and Marines. With the introduction of a four blade rotor system to the current Marine Sea Cobra, the AH-1W, the Bell Cobra is believed to have reached the limit of its development. While older Sea Cobra airframes can be brought up to AH-1W standards, the Marines view the need for a replacement for the Sea Cobra with some urgency.

The proposed Sea Apache (also known as the Gray Thunder) is intended for operations from smaller Navy ships such as frigates and cruisers and by the Marines from Amphibious Assault Ships (LHAs) and smaller helicopter capable amphibious ships of a Marine Amphibious Ready Group (ARG). These ships often operate outside the air cover of a carrier task group and the Sea Apache is also view as a limited air defense weapon and offensive surface strike platform.

Since 1984, several design studies and formal proposals have evolved with the Navy requesting changes in the Sea Apache configuration as it refined the aircraft's missions and roles. Each of the three proposed navalized versions of the Apache differed in several ways from the standard Army AH-64A, although all three proposals have the same powerplants in common, two 1,723 shp naval standard General Electric T700-GE-401 engines. Also in common are increased corrosion preventive measures, improved electro-magnetic interference protection, a Doppler navigation system, upgraded brakes, additional tie down points, and a powered automatic rotor blade fold system.

Originally, the Sea Apache was to be a basic AH-64A airframe modified with a folding tail boom, a relocated tail wheel, a mast mounted radar for surface/air search and attack, and provisions for Harpoon and Sidewinder missiles. Over time, however, the engineering studies and changing roles/missions requirements revealed that the Sea Apache's final configuration would have to be altered drastically.

One of the early problems encountered with navalizing the Apache was the narrow wheel base of the main landing gear. Engineering studies found that the standard Apache main wheel track was too narrow, causing the aircraft to be very unstable on the deck of a small ship. The roll of the deck in heavy seas, coupled with the aircraft's narrow wheel base, could easily cause the Sea Apache to tip over. To solve this problem, McDonnell Douglas engineers redesigned the main landing gear, relocating the landing gear from the fuselage to the tips of the stub wings. The revised main landing gear is also retractable, with the gear retracting into streamlined housings (although the wheel itself remains uncovered) on the end of each reinforced stub wing. These housings also have provisions for mounting Sidewinder missile launcher rails.

The revised landing gear configuration was put forward in the second proposal which also deleted the 30MM Chain Gun and its associated ammunition storage system, and replaced the TADS/PNVS with a nose mounted radar. The second Sea Apache featured a revised nose contour and extended fuselage side sponsons to carry additional electronics and fuel cells. The sponsons were smoothly faired into the fuselage to lower drag and extended almost to the tip of the nose. This aircraft was to also have provision for carrying two AIM-9L Sidewinder air-to-air missiles on short racks on the fuselage underside, a folding tail assembly and a retractable tail wheel.

The design has been refined still further, and the current Sea Apache proposal has the side fuselage sponsons deleted and a larger nose radome intended to house the APG-65 Sea Search radar. This radar, developed from the multi-mode radar used on the F/A-18

The U.S. Navy has shown an interest in acquiring the AH-64A in a navalized form to replace the AH-1 Sea Cobra. McDonnell Douglas' initial design study was a modified AH-64A equipped for duty aboard ship and armed with Sidewinders on each wing tip and four Harpoon anti-ship missiles. (McDonnell Douglas)

Hornet fighter/attack aircraft, is compatible for both air-to-surface attack and air-to-air engagements. The forward fuselage is deepened to house additional fuel cells and the relocated avionics bays.

Projected armament included both the Harpoon or Pengiun air-to-surface missiles (although the number of stations has been reduced to two) and two Sidewinder air-to-air missiles. To extend the Sea Apache's time on station, an in-flight refueling probe would be mounted on the starboard fuselage side below the cockpit. Consideration is also being given to installing the Canadian developed Bear Trap automatic haul-down landing system, which allows operations during heavy sea states.

One proposed Marine Corps variant would retain the TADS/PNVS and Hellfire missile system, for use in the close air support role and for anti-shipping duties while escorting amphibious vessels. This aircraft would relocate the radar dome back to the top of the rotor mast. Another option favored by the Marines is the capability to use the four tube TOW missile system as a back-up to the Hellfire missile system.

Some of the missions envisioned by the Navy for the Sea Apache are; escort for amphibious assault craft, anti-shipping strike, Combat Air Patrol (CAP) with up to six Sidewinders, Over the Horizon (OTH) targeting for surface ships, air support for SEAL special warfare teams, standoff surveillance, and long range coastal patrol.

The Harpoon is an air breathing, turbo-jet engine powered, all weather, over-the-horizon anti-ship missile. The Harpoon, like the French Exocet (AM.39), is a low level cruise type missile that employs active radar guidance and a high explosive warhead. (McDonnell Douglas)

Sea Apache Evolution

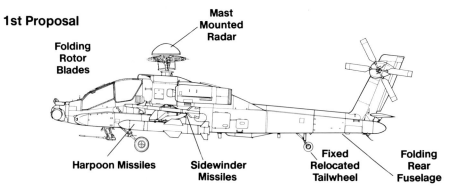

1st Proposal
- Mast Mounted Radar
- Folding Rotor Blades
- Harpoon Missiles
- Sidewinder Missiles
- Fixed Relocated Tailwheel
- Folding Rear Fuselage

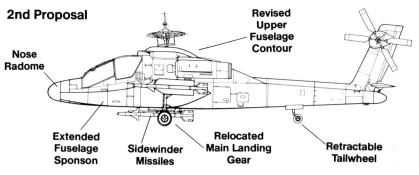

2nd Proposal
- Revised Upper Fuselage Contour
- Nose Radome
- Extended Fuselage Sponson
- Sidewinder Missiles
- Relocated Main Landing Gear
- Retractable Tailwheel

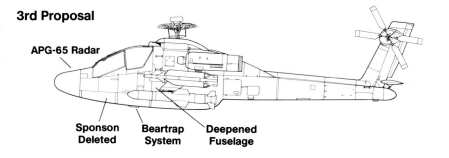

3rd Proposal
- APG-65 Radar
- Sponson Deleted
- Beartrap System
- Deepened Fuselage

Marine variants are planned to be used as escorts for troop-carrying helicopters, close air support for landing forces, anti-armor support, Forward Air Control (FAC) for artillery and Naval gunfire spotting. The Marines view the Sea Apache as the best available replacement for the Sea Cobra. The Sea Apache would give the commander of an Amphibious Ready Group (ARG) a dedicated attack/limited air defense aircraft readily available stationed aboard the LHA/LPH/LPD classes of assault ships in his task force (this mission currently can only be partially covered by the AH-1W Sea Cobra and usually requires stationing a flight of Harriers aboard the LHA).

Weapons planned for use with the Sea Apache include Harpoon, Stinger, Sidewinder, Sidearm, AMRAAM, Penguin, and Hellfire missiles, as well as 5 inch Zuni and 2.75 inch FFAR rockets. The Harpoon, Penguin and Hellfire missiles would be used against large naval targets, the Sidewinder and Stinger in the air-to-air mode, and the 5 inch Zuni and 2.75 inch FFAR rockets against smaller water borne targets and ground targets. A variety of missiles/rockets could be carried at the same time giving the Sea Apache the capability of engaging different types of targets on the same mission, making it a very versatile and useful naval aircraft.

Performance goals specified for the Sea Apache by the Navy include a 200 nautical mile mission radius, and a four hour endurance on station.

Currently, the Navy is giving serious consideration to the purchase of the Sea Apache once adequate funding is made available to finance prototype construction. The Navy desires the Sea Apache not only for its capabilities, but also because the aircraft would cost far less to acquire than to undertake the design of a totally new aircraft to replace the AH-1Ws in service.

In response to Navy requirements, McDonnell Douglas modified the Sea Apache proposal with a new nose area housing upgraded electronics, relocated landing gear, and the cannon deleted. The Sea Apache has also been nicknamed Gray Thunder because of its overall Light Gray camouflage scheme. (McDonnell Douglas)

The final proposal for the Sea Apache calls for a deepened fuselage, a further modification to the nose section to incorporate a radar from an F/A-18 Hornet, and an inflight refueling probe. The projected missions for the Sea Apache include; anti-shipping, anti-air, combat search and rescue escort, naval gunfire spotting and forward air control. (McDonnell Douglas)

Multi-Stage Improvement Program/ Advanced Apache(AH-64B)

As part of the Apache program, the Army has undertaken a Multi-Stage Improvement Program (MSIP) which upgrades the Apache's capabilities as technology is advanced and new equipment developed. Some of these improvements, such as an upgraded IR suppression system and fuselage mounted wire cutters are currently being fitted to late production AH-64As on the production line while field modification kits are being produced to retrofit earlier Apaches to the current production standard.

Problems that surfaced during early service deployment of the Apache, such as gun jamming due to weak motor sheer pins, ammunition binding in the ammunition carrier, and premature failure of some hydraulic lines have been corrected. The sheer pin problem has been corrected by replacing the sheer pins with stronger units capable of withstanding higher stress loads. The ammunition carrier problem was solved by development of an improved ammunition carrier which is currently being retrofitted to all Apaches in service. The hydraulic line problem has also been solved and the older lines are also being replaced using field modification kits supplied by McDonnell Douglas.

Systems upgrades planned under the MSIP include an upgraded fire control computer, larger forward avionics bay, capability to utilize the Global Positioning Satellite for navigation, an improved Helmet Display Unit, improved hover augmentation system, improved pressurized air conditioning system, and enhancements of the Apache's air-to-air capabilities.

Defensive air-to-air capability for the Apache currently rests in tube mounted Stingers (two and four tube racks) and Sidewinders carried on the outboard weapons pylons. While effective, these limit the amount of air-to-ground weapons that can be carried. To cure this problem the Apache will be fitted with the air-to-air Stinger system (ATAS). The light weight of the system (103 pounds) allows the Apache to mount the launchers on wing tips freeing the underwing pylons for air-to-ground weapons. Each launcher will carry two (with an option for four) ATAS tubes. The Stinger, being an infrared guided missile, is simple to operate. Once the target is located the system is activated by either the copilot/gunner or the pilot and the Apache is maneuvered to position the target in the missile seeker's field of view. When the missile is fired the Apache is free to engage other targets.

The ATAS was successfully test fired from an Apache at the Yuma Test Range and McDonnell Douglas is now engaged in final development work on the missile control systems for the Apache. Additional tests, including live fire tests, are scheduled to be conducted with the system during 1990, with service introduction following shortly thereafter.

Another improvement being undertaked under the MSIP is development of a Wire Strike Protection System (WSPS) to protect the Apache from damage caused by flying into electrical and telephone wires during low level operations. Wire stike is a serious problem that accounts for a high percentage of helicopter losses, especially during nap-of-the-earth flight.

The Wire Strike Protection System was developed by Bristol Aerospace in Winnipeg, Canada. Under the Army development contract, worth some 3.4 million dollars and administered by the Army Avaition Systems Command, a production AH-64A was delivered to Bristol for prototype mounting hardware installation design. Bristol has completed this portion of the contract and has supplied McDonnell Douglas with the necessary information to modify the AH-64 with a complete Wire Stike Protection System.

The development contract calls for two sets of WSPS equipment to be installed on AH-64As loaned to McDonnell Douglas by the Army with the installation work being undertaken at the McDonnell Douglas Mesa facility. One aircraft will be retained at

McDonnell Douglas for company flight tests while the second aircraft will be tested by the Army Aviation Applied Technology Directorate at Fort Eustis, Virgnia.

The system consists of wire deflectors and wire cutters located at various positions on the aircraft. Deflectors are placed on the TADS/PNVS turret, windshield, around the cannon, the lower fuselage jack pad, and in front of the tail wheel. Wire cutters are located on the nose, canopy framing, fuselage top, main landing gear mounts, and above the cannon.

After tests at Fort Eustis, the aircraft will be delivered to the National Aeronautics and Space Administration's Langley, Virginia test facility for swing tests. During this series of tests the Apache will be suspended from a 200 foot tower and swung through a variety of wire types at speeds of forty to fifty mph. If the system passes all tests, the Army intends to install the WSPS equipment on Apaches on the production line and purchase field modification kits to upgrade all AH-64As in service.

Advanced Apache (AH-64B)

An improved version of the AH-64A is currently under development under the McDonnell-Douglas designation, Advanced Apache (although it is expected that the Army will give this aircraft the designation AH-64B in the near future). The majority of improvements intended for the Advanced Apache/AH-64B are in the areas of visionics, electronics, and avionics, with structural improvements for the airframe and wing being

Normal armament loads for the Apache consist of eight Hellfire missiles on the inboard weapons pylons and two 2.75 inch rocket pods on the outer pylons. The bulged forward equipment bay doors identify this Apache as a late production aircraft. (U.A. Army)

confined to graphite/epoxy composite airframe sections to reduce weight and a wet wing (i.e. a wing with an intergal fuel tank installed). The wet wing, when fully loaded, would extend the Apache's range to 3,100 nautical miles on internal fuel. Use of a wet wing would free up weapons stations while giving the Apache the extended range normally associated with external fuel tanks. The increase in range would allow the Army to deploy Apaches to Europe using the southern ferry route thrugh the Azores Isands, taking advantage of the better weather along this route.

Crew survivability has been given special consideration and the Advanced Apache is equipped with an improved crew compartment air filtration system, along with an aircrew warning system to warn of chemical or biological contamination. An improved air conditioned environment will be installed to cool the crew while they are wearing protective clothing in a CBR (chemical, biological, radiological) environment. Attention has also been given to crew eye protection from battlefield laser light in the form of a special helmet visor.

Further attention has been given to the total elimination of all mechanical push-rods and bell cranks in the existing flight controls. These will be replaced by an electronic flight control system (fly-by-wire) that uses a side stick controller similar to that used in the General Dynamics F-16.

The Advanced Apache/AH-64B will utilize a total "glass cockpit" concept (i.e. replacement of standard instrumentation with video units) totally in the copilot/gunners station and make more use of improved Helmet Mounted Display Systems. Electronic control functions are improved through the use of a voice interactive system, touch screen overlays on the multi-function display video panel, a cursor control, and a full alpha/numeric keyboard to update the various computer systems to changing battlefield conditions.

One computer program to be installed into the Apache's fire control computer will intergrate automatic operation of the IR jammer, radar warning system, and missile warning system. This new program will also be used in conjunction with new sensors to provide the crew with an audible warning of when they are being illuminated by a laser targeting system.

Another improvement intended for the Advanced Apache/AH-64B is the Martin Marietta/Westinghouse Airborne Adverse Weather Weapons System (AAWWS), a mast mounted millimeter wavelength radar system. The 175 pound radar dome (total systems weight is 230 pounds) is mounted above the rotor mast and is coupled with a cockpit display that will give the pilot many of the normal features of a standard search radar, including target recognition, air-to-air and air-to-ground targeting, and limited terrain contour mapping.

The Hellfire missile is also being modified with a new thirty pound, millimeter wave seeker head that will give the Hellfire a fire and forget capability. Once a target has been detected by the AAWWS, the copilot/gunner would boresight/lock the missile seeker onto the target and fire the missile. Once launched, the Hellfire will guide to the target using its own radar.

Currently the program is in the development stage with a mock-up installation being flight tested on two standard AH-64As and full systems tests with an operational system being planned for late 1989.

Funded under the MSIP program, four prototypes of improved AH-64As will be built incorporating most of the features (except for the glass cockpit and structural changes) of the MISP/Advanced Apache, with the first flight expected during July of 1991. If the program successfully passes all tests, the Army envisions operational deployment of AAWWS configured AH-64s during late 1992.

Additional weapons are also being considered for installation on the Advanced Apache. McDonnell Doulgas is currently investigating installation of the Harm anti-radiation missile, the Chaparral air-to-air missile system, and a new air-to-air system being developed by Shorts of England, the Starstreak.

The Starstreak missile system is a unique system that consists of a tube-launched, hyper-velocity missile capable of speeds up to Mach 4.5. The missile itself consists of a center body propulsion system with three high kenetic energy explosive darts as the missile warhead. The three darts are released after sustainer burn out and continue on to the target in a tight formation for the greatest probablity of a direct hit. The missile uses a laser guidance system that is compatible with the laser designator of the Apache. Operationally, the missile would be carried in four tube launchers mounted on the Apache wing tip, similar to the Stinger system.

The Army is currently testing a mock-up of the mast-mounted radar on this late production Apache. The radar system will be used with a new Hellfire active radar seeker head which will give the weapons system a true fire and forget mode of operation.

Wire Strike Protection System

MISP AH-64A/ Advanced Apache

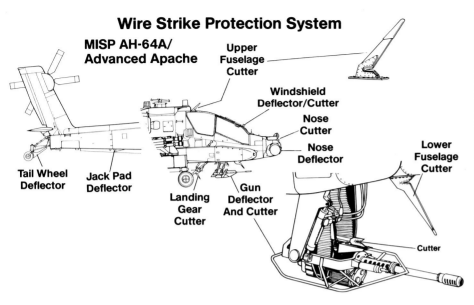

Upper Fuselage Cutter

Windshield Deflector/Cutter

Nose Cutter

Nose Deflector

Lower Fuselage Cutter

Tail Wheel Deflector

Jack Pad Deflector

Landing Gear Cutter

Gun Deflector And Cutter

Cutter

A pair of late production AH-64As on the ramp at Naval Air Station Dallas, Texas, during October of 1988. Both aircraft are equipped with the Wire Strike Protection System. Most Apaches currently equipped with the WSPS are slated for duty in Europe. (China Clipper Photo)

The metal framework around the 30mm cannon on this late production AH-64 is part of the Wire Strike Protection System. The pointed metal objects on the landing gear legs and under the fuselage in front of the gun are wire cutters designed to sever any telephone/electrical lines that the Apache might fly into. (China Clipper Photo)

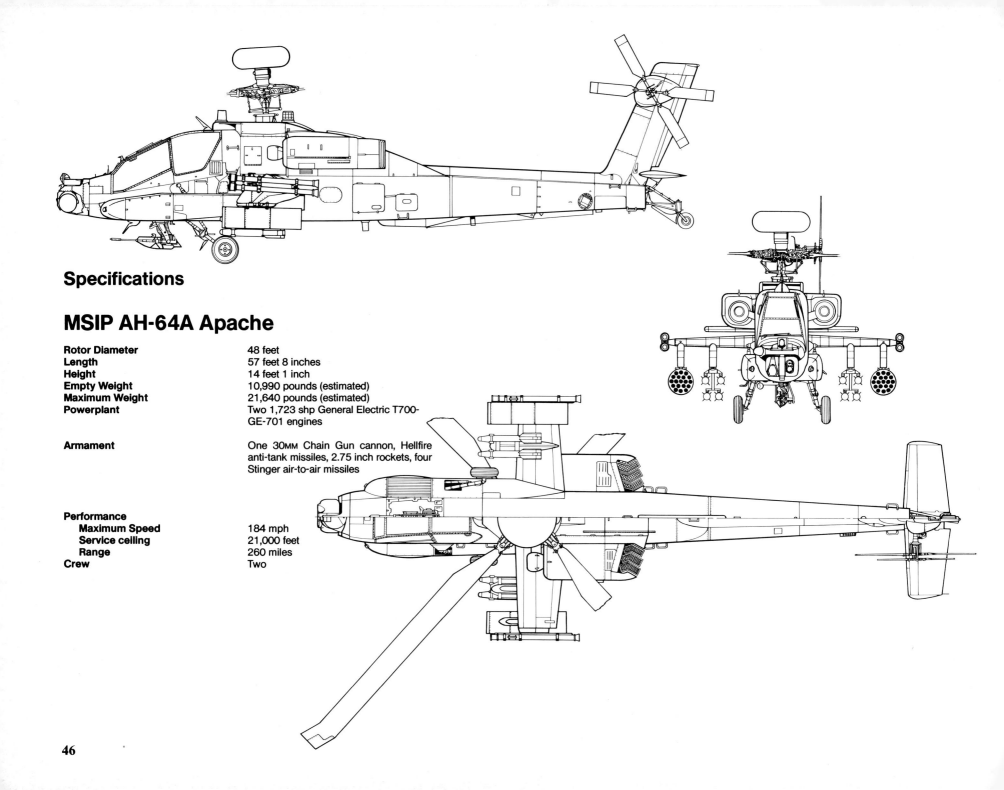

Specifications

MSIP AH-64A Apache

Rotor Diameter	48 feet
Length	57 feet 8 inches
Height	14 feet 1 inch
Empty Weight	10,990 pounds (estimated)
Maximum Weight	21,640 pounds (estimated)
Powerplant	Two 1,723 shp General Electric T700-GE-701 engines
Armament	One 30mm Chain Gun cannon, Hellfire anti-tank missiles, 2.75 inch rockets, four Stinger air-to-air missiles
Performance	
Maximum Speed	184 mph
Service ceiling	21,000 feet
Range	260 miles
Crew	Two

This late production Apache (86-9002) is also equipped with the Wire Strike Protection System. The WSPS uses deflectors and cutters to protect the Apache from damage caused by one of the major dangers to low-flying helicopters, — telephone and electrical power lines. (China Clipper Photo)

The main rotor blades of this Apache have been secured by tie downs to prevent the wind from causing the blades to flap. The tie down system consists of nylon bags that slide over the rotor tips and nylon lines that run from the rotor tips to the fuselage, securing the rotors in place. (China Clipper Photo)

Wingtip Stinger Missile Mount

MISP AH-64A/
Advanced Apache

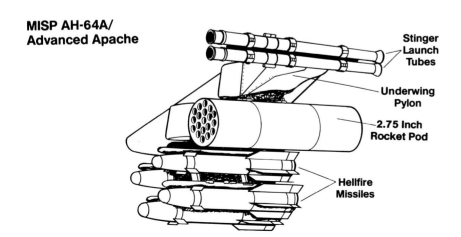

Stinger Launch Tubes

Underwing Pylon

2.75 Inch Rocket Pod

Hellfire Missiles

LHX

Originally conceived by the U.S. Army as a replacement for the Bell OH-58 Scout and Bell AH-1 Cobra, the LHX (Light Helicopter Experimental) was to be developed in two different versions, a light scout/utility aircraft and a light single-seat attack variant. The LHX is to be in the 7,000 pound empty weight class and will be powered by the new GE T800 engine. Two contractor teams have been working on the LHX program since its inception during 1983, McDonnell Douglas/Bell and Boeing/Sikorsky. Each have made several proposals and delivered several design studies to the U.S. Army, none of which have been accepted. This is primarily due to changes in configuration and a change in Army Aviation budgeting policies, which limited the program's funding.

Army planning currently calls for the LHX to be a two seat scout/attack helicopter with state-of-the-art electronics, a NOTAR (no tail rotor) system, and an advanced bearingless main rotor system. Army program requirements for the LHX are strict. The aircraft's weight is limited to 7,300 pounds (empty) and the unit fly-away cost has a ceiling of $7.5 million dollars. If the program reaches the full scale development stage, competative prototyes will be built by each of the two main contractor teams.

During early 1988, the LHX Program and its funds for prototype development were severely curtailed. Initially the program was aimed at a possible 60 billion dollar, 7,000 unit purchase. Today the program is limited to a 160 million dollar developmental fund to build prototypes of the two seat scout/attack variant during 1990 (although a utility variant remains as an option to replace the OH-58D). First flight for the scout/attack version is expected to take place during 1995.

The two contractor teams involved in the LHX program are Boeing/Sikorsky and McDonnell Douglas/Bell. As part of the test program, McDonnell Douglas has been

The latest LHX proposal made by MDHC features a pilot and copilot/gunner seated in tandem under a blown cockpit canopy. The aircraft uses the NOTAR system and a conventional tail plane. The LHX would be armed with a large caliber chain gun, anti-tank missiles, and air-to-air missiles for self-defense. (McDonnell Douglas)

using one of the original Apache prototypes (YAH-64 AV-05) as an electronics test bed to test the various avionics, electronics, and visionic components that are to be used in the LHX. The front cockpit of the YAH-64 has been reconfigured as a "glass cockpit", consisting of visual display units (VDU) for all engine, avionics, weapons, and navigational instruments. This totally integrated instrument panel will be utilized in conjunction with an advanced helmet display unit that is presently undergoing upgrading for the Advanced Apache program.

The modified Apache is also fitted with an advanced fly-by-wire control system (also intended for the Advanced Apache) and has the PNVS turret removed with the opening faired over. It carries a large test probe mounted on the port side below the cockpit and is normally flown with the stub wings removed.

The YAH-64 (84-28258) has been painted with the silhouette of the proposed LHX airframe on the side of the Apache. The stylized paint scheme is in the McDonnell Douglas Helicopter colors of Blue and Silver against the standard Army Field Green camouflage.

Two other aircraft involved in the LHX development test program are the McDonnell Douglas NOTAR OH-6 prototype and a Bell 222 demonstrator fitted with the bearingless main rotor system. The NOTAR prototype is a highly modified McDonnell Douglas OH-6A which uses ducted air which is forced under pressure through a series of slots in the rear fuselage to provide the anti-torque forces. Directional control is accomplished by means of a rotating directional control thruster mounted at the end of the tail boom. The NOTAR system prototype has flown more than 400 hours and has demonstrated maneuvers far beyond the capabilities of conventional tail rotor helicopters. Advantages to the NOTAR system include; superior handling qualities, reduced weight (by elimination of the tail rotor, gear boxes, drive shafts, etc), reduced maintenance, increased safety (both on the ground and in the air), increased reliability, and lower costs.

McDonnell Douglas is currently developing a new civil helicopter, the MDX, which utilizes the NOTAR system. Since its announcement in January of 1989, over 175 have been placed for this new state-of-the-art helicopter, even though the prototype's first flight is not expected until May of 1992. Experience gained with the MDX project will directly benefit the LHX program which will use a lot of the same airframe technology.

The Sikorsky/Bell proposal would be equipped with similar armament to that carried by the MDHC/Bell LHX, with the missiles being housed internally in the stub wings. The LHX is intended to replace the AH-1, UH-1 and OH-58, and will take advantage of the latest technology in glass instrument panels, avionics, and visionic. (U.S. Army)

A McDonnell Douglas MD 500 series helicopter has been configured with the no tail rotor (NOTAR) design. Without the tail rotor, the noise signature of the so equipped helicopter is significantly reduced. The NOTAR system operates by directing pressurized air through horizontal slots along the boom to counteract rotor torque, thereby eliminating the tail rotor. (McDonnell Douglas)

YAH-64 (AV-05) has been modified to serve as a test bed for the various avionics, electronics, and visionics components that will be used on the MDHC/Bell LHX program. The YAH-64 is painted with a stylized LHX silhouette in Silver over the standard Army Field Green camouflage. (McDonnell Douglas)

ARMY AVIATION
From
Squadron/Signal

1075

1087

1091

1092

 **squadron/signal publications**